D1571949

Aids to "Revelation"

Aids
to
"Revelation"

WATCHMAN NEE

Translated from the Chinese

**Christian Fellowship Publishers, Inc.
New York**

ISBN 0-935008-60-8

Available from the Publishers at:

11515 Allecingie Parkway
Richmond, Virginia 23235

PRINTED IN U.S.A.

TRANSLATOR'S PREFACE

As we are quickly approaching the close of this age with the blessed hope in view of the dawning of a new age — even the millennium, it is no surprise that the hearts of God's children are increasingly drawn to the last book of the Bible, Revelation. Whereas in the past that book was shunned by most as not being understandable; now it is looked upon as a blessed book, just as it is written of it: "Blessed is he that readeth, and they that hear the words of the prophecy, and keep the things that are written therein: for the time is at hand" (Rev. 1.3).

In the study of Revelation, however, there are certain basic things one must know in order to understand this book. The lack of such fundamental knowledge has kept people in the past from reading it and it still presents a problem to those who are now studying it. In order to encourage God's children to study, Watchman Nee in the nineteen-twenties prepared aids to the book of Revelation and published them in serial form in *Christian* Magazine, from Volume 2 to Volume 23. Although these writings belong to his early days, the light released remains nonetheless undiminished through the years since that time. They offer invaluable helps to all who love the word of God.

In this present volume, then, the author deals with the attitude the believers should have towards the book of Revelation as well as the ways and means of

understanding it. He presents the different schools of
interpretation concerning Revelation and offers the
key to its right interpretation. He touches upon the
distinction between salvation and reward, the four
kinds of judgment, and the spiritual significance of
numerals in the Bible since these are essential to
rightly dividing the word of truth. He compares the
prophecies in Revelation with the other prophecies of
the Bible—such as Daniel's human image and the
seventy sevens, the Olivet prophecy of our Lord, and
Paul's prophecy found in 2 Thessalonians. Finally, he
summarizes the great events of the future as given in
Revelation according to their respective times, and
suggests a detailed outline of the book.

May the Lord use this volume to help many to
read, to hearken, and to keep the things written in the
book of Revelation.

CONTENTS

1 | Introduction

The book of Revelation is the very last one in the Bible. It is the consummation of God's revelation and the conclusion of God's word. Without this portion of God's word the Bible would become a book without an ending, and many of the problems in other books of the Bible would remain unsolved also. How sad that to many of God's children this book does not seem to exist in their Bible! They neither read nor understand it. This is one of the reasons for the spiritual weakness prevailing among God's people.

The pages of Revelation constitute the record of the fulfillment of all promises and prophecies. It follows the Law, the Prophets, the Psalms, the Gospels, and the Epistles. It implements the types and completes the teachings of the aforementioned writings. It is the last message given by the Lord Jesus to His Church to show forth His relationships with His Church, His Israel, and His enemy. It is a book of wars: the war between Christ and the Antichrist;

between God and Satan. This book reveals how the saints will stand with the Lord in one mind to resist Satan and his hosts. Yet if this be true in the future, how much more it ought to be true today. May the Lord give us grace that at the present we may assume the attitude of conqueror against the devil; that in faith we will resist him in our lives and deeds; and that we will deepen our own enmity towards him.

It is most fitting that the book of Revelation was placed at the end of the New Testament. When we read the Gospels, we will no doubt think of the future kingdom of God and its glory. As we read the Epistles, our expectation for the future is undoubtedly intensified. It appears that the entire Bible is pointing to that future to which our Christian hearts are drawn. But then, the book of Revelation concludes all the earlier prophecies pronounced and lays the future agenda before us, causing us to know most assuredly that one day the creation will groan no more and the believers will suffer no more!

How appropriate all this is. What the saints have experienced in the world increases their longing for the coming of that day. How numerous are the sins of the world, how prevailing are its violences. Yet how the saints look forward to the triumph of righteousness and truth! The book of Revelation speaks of the coming judgment by God of evil as well as declares the final victory of the lovers of God. See how merciful is the Lord: He gives us this book to comfort and to satisfy us. How He always cares for us!

The Lord Jesus Christ is the center of God's word

(cf. Luke 24.27, John 5.39). Hence He is the key to the word of God. Either directly or indirectly, the whole Bible speaks of Him. It points to Jesus and revolves around Him. Take Him out, and no one can understand the Bible at all. "In the roll of the book it is written of me" (Heb. 10.7). Martin Luther once said that in the world "there is only one book—the Bible, only one person—Jesus Christ." The Lord Jesus Christ is the detail as well as the outline of the Bible. If we read the message of Revelation with a heart that seeks after Christ, we shall see in every page His face and hear from every page His voice. This book, as do all the other books of the Bible, takes the person of Christ as the subject and the glory of Christ as the object. If we do not see Christ in the pages of Revelation, then all that we see will be vanity. By drawing near to this book, we draw near to Christ. How beautiful that is!

May we receive much grace to see more of Christ in all the pages of this book. How deplorable that commentators as well as readers care a great deal about the judgments, symbols, mysteries and consequences of this book but forget that Christ is our beloved Lord! May He enable us to seek Him with a single mind and exalt Him above all else. May we learn to love and obey Him more and more.

From the very outset Revelation records the person and work of the Lord Jesus. Many names are given in the first chapter; and all these reveal His person—His deity. It speaks of His life on earth in terms of His being "the faithful witness" (1.5); it speaks of His substitutionary death on the cross in

the following ways: "loosed us from our sins by his
blood" (1.5), "I was dead" (1.18), "a Lamb . . . as
though it had been slain" (5.6), and "Worthy is the
Lamb that hath been slain" (5.12). This book mentions Him as the Lamb 28 times, and in each instance
it causes us to remember how He has died for our
sins. How much He loves us indeed (1.5). But His
resurrection is also recorded in this book in ways such
as "the firstborn of the dead" (1.5), "the Living one;
and I was dead, and behold, I am alive for evermore"
(1.18), and "the first and the last, who was dead and
lived again" (2.8).

Because of Christ's death and resurrection, God
the Father has given Him incomparably the greatest
glory, as Paul so eloquently tells us: "he humbled
himself, becoming obedient even unto death, yea, the
death of the cross. *Wherefore* also God highly exalted
him, and gave unto him the name which is above
every name; that in the name of Jesus every knee
should bow, of things in heaven and things on earth
and things under the earth, and that every tongue
should confess that Jesus Christ is Lord, to the glory
of God the Father" (Phil. 2.8–11). We notice how the
words of these verses from the Epistles are fulfilled in
this last book of the Bible. Revelation tells us how He
will receive the praises of the redeemed, the acclama-
tions of the angelic hosts, and the worship of all creation. May the hearts of all who love the Lord be lifted
up, for we rejoice in seeing Him glorified.

A large portion of this book is devoted to Christ's
judgment, in accordance with John 5: "For neither
doth the Father judge any man, but he hath given all

judgment unto the Son" (v.22). Who is able to stand against the wrath of the Lamb? There is nothing which our Lord does that is not proper. His beauty is fully manifested both in His favor and in His wrath; and that causes us to admire Him all the more. Formerly He was so humble! How despised and ill-treated by men He was! But now, He is full of majesty and glory! May the Lord enable us to see His honor in these terrible judgments. After Revelation chapter 19, we come to see how He is united in one with His bride, how He destroys all who oppose Him, how the victorious believers reign with Him for a thousand years, and how He looks after His own in the new heaven and the new earth. Truly, the Lord Jesus is *the* theme of the book of Revelation. If the word of God does indeed take Christ as its center, then how we ought to make Him the center of our speech and our walk. Since God has given everything to Him, then we must give Him our all in both our words and deeds.

Now besides the person and glory of Christ, this book also takes up—as its secondary concern—the Church and the kingdom, yet not as separated from but as joined to Christ. In this book, as we have said, the world is under judgment; so that as far as this world is concerned, Revelation records nothing of it but judgment. And concerning the Church in this world, the book may not give any account of her special privileges but it does say something of her responsibility. Nevertheless, what the Old Testament does not mention about the heavenly aspect of the Church and the glory of the kingdom are things

clearly disclosed in this last portion of the New
Testament.

In Revelation God is presented as the Judge of
this age, and Christ is portrayed as the Executor.
Judgment begins with the house of God and ulti-
mately reaches out to the world. In this book the
Holy Spirit is revealed as "the seven Spirits" instead
of the "one Spirit" that is presented in other books of
the Bible, simply because He is spoken of in accordance with the work of the government of God.

Do let us realize that the book of Revelation is not
one of secrecy but one of disclosure. If it were a
sealed book, we would have no hope of understanding it. But since it is a book of *revelation* we need to
ask the Spirit of God to teach us so that we may
know. The basic meaning of "revelation" is "an
unveiling." And hence, the Holy Spirit unveils to us
in this book the glory and the person of the Lord
Jesus. May He open our eyes to behold the precious
teaching within its pages.

2 | Why the Book of Revelation Is Neglected

Genesis is the first book in the Bible, and it tells of God's curse upon Satan. Revelation is the last book in the Bible, and it reveals how Satan is defeated in the future and how God executes judgment against him. The original face of Satan and his eternal ending are recorded in these two books. For this reason, Satan harbors a special hatred towards them. He attacks Genesis by suggesting that its record does not agree with the findings of science, and that therefore the story of creation found in it is but a myth. Outwardly he appears to assail the record of the creation story, but actually he tries to cover up the history of his own curse. Against the book of Revelation—which predicts his end—he adopts another approach of attack. Instead of openly assailing it, he attempts to turn it into a sealed book. He insinuates that its pages are so profound and its recorded future events so difficult to understand that it would be a waste of time to study it. Hence many

believers have never even touched this book. And thus
he easily covers up his future disgrace!

Revelation was not only despised but even rejected
by Christians in former times. This we know from a
study of Church history. In today's twentieth century,
though some Christians — very few in number — are willing to read it, ordinary believers — the vast majority —
are generally lukewarm towards it. Many, as it were,
put this book "on the shelf." Some do not read it
because they do not even read the other books of the
Bible; others, because they do not rely upon the Holy
Spirit and have no patience to read it. How often we
hear people say: "This book is too profound, too
mysterious for me to read."

The fact of the matter is there are many significant
reasons why Revelation is not welcome but is often a
stumbling block to many. Briefly stated, besides the
Satanic obstruction already mentioned, it may be said
that the contents of this book do not easily create in
worldly believers any good feelings. It does indeed
speak of the glory of the future millennial kingdom
and the joy of the eternal kingdom, all of which are
true and certain (ch. 20.1-9, chs. 21-22.5). But those
who will enjoy such glory and joy need to be "faithful
unto death" (2.10), and "hold fast till I come" (2.25).
They must "watch," "repent," and "be zealous." In
order to gain the future world, they must forsake this
present world. Now is the suffering, but then is to be
the glory. Otherwise, whoever has the glory of the
world today will suffer shame in the future world.
Many carnal believers find it difficult to cut their tie

with the world which they have loved too long. Since the reading of Revelation will therefore produce anxiety and distress, they have decided not to read it.

Another explanation for why Revelation is an unwelcome part of the Bible centers around the fact that a large portion of the book deals with God's wrath and judgment (see chs. 4–19). People like to hear about the love of God. The ideal god of men is one who never gets angry and never ever judges. Nevertheless, this book speaks of the righteousness of God eventuating in His wrath and His judgment — divine activities that are always unwelcome by all men. Who, then, would be willing to read about such matters?

Another reason is that from the beginning to the end, the pages of Revelation deal with all kinds of supernatural phenomena. God knows men only care for natural occurrences, but He wants us to come face to face with Him. Hence He will deal with us on supernatural ground. People may tolerate reading about the supernatural events of the past because these can have no effect upon them since these events have already passed and situations have also changed. But if in the future such supernatural phenomena are yet to come to pass, these will strike deadly blows to their materialism and their scorn of miracles and wonders. And if such occurrences are truly to come in the future, should they not then live piously today on earth and glory in God? How pitiable that many try to spiritualize this book away because they cannot bear the simple but horrendous teachings found in it. They take it all as allegorical in nature without it having any real

historical value for them in the future. How the flesh
shies away from the two-edged sword of God! How
deceitful above all things is the human heart!

Many people deem the world to be getting better
every day. Is not civilization making progress daily?
They think the world is heading upward and forward,
without any sign of regression. And in accordance with
such acceleration in progress, they muse that very soon
the ideal Christian society will appear on earth. Yet
how different is the word of Revelation from men's
thoughts! It never for a moment considers the world
as progressive! Rather, its testimony is that the sins of
men will have increased so rapidly that the world stands
irredeemable because it rejects God and His salvation.
And hence, apart from judgment, there is nothing else
to be done; for even with the severest judgment, men
will not repent. This is true not only with the world
but even with the Church! The Church has left her first
love; therefore she will be "spewed out" by the Lord.
The modern conception of things and God's word are
totally at variance. Since the words of Revelation bear
witness to God and not to man, it is not agreeable to
men's thought, and consequently it is not welcome by
men. How deplorable that many have lost the spirit
of testifying against the sinfulness of this world, just
as the pages of Revelation show!

The position which the true Church should arrive
at is yet another explanation for why people do not
like to read the pages of this book. What Revelation
chapters 2 and 3 speak concerning the true condition
of the Church distresses those many believers who still
love the world. Modern men stress work. If there are

to be many activities, then these Christians will be reckoned as "tops." Yet Revelation judges it to be useless if there are many activities but no first love. Anybody who is truly for the Lord must be "faithful unto death" and must be "watchful." This is something worldly believers cannot bear.

A final reason for the unpopularity of Revelation among many is that there is a modern conception that calls for the entire world to be saved in the future. Yet Revelation speaks against such a misconception as this. On the contrary, it predicts that in the future countless numbers of people will be eternally lost in "the lake of fire." Those who imagine themselves to be more compassionate than God will most surely resist its teaching. They would like to think that the punishment of sinners is but for a time and then there will simply be their annihilation. But once again the book of Revelation is opposed to such wishful thinking. It shows that the sufferings of the lake of fire are everlasting — without end. Since this book is full of woes, plagues, curses, distresses, and warnings, it is not surprising that people will not read it, welcome it or accept it.

To sum up, the book of Revelation, in its teachings, is so opposite to human thought that few will study it even today. But there *are* those few who do take the trouble to read its pages.

The saints who love the Lord take a very different attitude towards this book. They find in its words a supply in time of lack, support in time of despair, comfort in time of sorrow, succour in time of weakness. This volume wipes away their tears, increases their faith, and revives their will. How those saints who are willing to suffer for the Lord love to read its pages! For Christ's sake, they become poor and lonely. They walk the narrow way of the cross. Yet in their distresses, they find solace in Revelation, they discover great hope in it; for will not the second coming of the Lord gladden those who love His appearing? However great the afflictions on earth may be, the hope of being raptured to heaven more than compensates for them all. How can we fail to admire the New Jerusalem, the City of Gold? Though much has to be forsaken today, the gain in *that* day when we shall reign with Christ will be so much greater. The present afflictions are light and momentary in comparison with the eternal glory of the coming kingdom (cf. Rom. 8.18, 2 Cor. 4.17). The book of Revelation is truly a blessing to Christians.

3 | How We Can Understand "Revelation"

To understand the book of Revelation, the first thing one must do is to *read* it. Without doing this, none can understand it. Is it not strange that when believers are asked why they do not read Revelation their answer is because they do not understand it! Do they mean to say that one must understand its pages first and then read it?!? May God grant us patience to study His word so that we do not quit reading as soon as we meet some difficulty and thus lose out on many blessings. Whoever reads this book of Revelation should not rely simply on his own mental power; he should prayerfully, humbly and openly ask for the illumination of the Holy Spirit. When His light shines upon the word of God, things that have not been understood for many years past will immediately be comprehended.

Furthermore, the reader of this book must keep his heart pure—that is to say, he is not to read it out of curiosity concerning future events. He ought instead to peruse its pages with the desire to know more of God's word so that he may keep God's will and may receive whatever He intends to give through His word. God will not bless if the reading merely serves to garner more food for a curious mind, for that will not profit our spiritual life.

In my view, the first thing to do towards grasping hold of the book of Revelation is to gain a thorough knowledge of it. At the start, read it chapter by chapter. Read till you can remember the contents of each chapter without looking at it. Then read carefully verse by verse. Memorize the verses you consider important. Use all kinds of methods to make yourself thoroughly acquainted with this volume. As you become familiar with its contents, the Holy Spirit will then be able to teach you.

Now once being fully acquainted with the book, you will soon discover its natural divisions. You will be able to perceive its method and to decide which part is main history and which part is parenthesis. You can then put the main history in order and determine the relationship between history and parenthesis. With a program of detailed study such as this, you will come to see which part is clearly explained and which part is only implied. There is no problem with the portions that are explained, but with the implied portions, one must compare it with other sections of the Scriptures. Since the book of Revelation is the sum total of the entire Bible (in that it concludes all the unconcluded problems to be found in the preceding books of the Bible), we should search the other biblical books to ferret out all the pertinent connections. By interpreting

Scripture with Scripture, we will arrive at an accurate explanation and understanding. Yet, as we have already observed, reading the Bible is not for knowledge, it is for the cultivation of spiritual life. And hence, even with the understandable parts we need to ask the Holy Spirit to show us their spiritual meanings so as to receive spiritual help.

4 | The Time "Revelation" Was Written

The period when Revelation was written constitutes a serious problem, in part because some Rationalistic teachers have advocated an earlier date for its composition — they asserting that probably it was at the time of the reign of the Roman Emperor Nero. They have formulated this particular time frame in order to establish the theory that the serious proclamations recorded in the book of Revelation were all fulfilled after the infamous and devastating fire that took place in Rome in Nero's time. According to this theory, what the book prophecied actually pointed only to the persecutions of the Christians of old and the destruction of Jerusalem together with events which occurred at that very period of Roman history. The prophecy concerning the beast or the Antichrist simply has reference to the tyranny and evil deeds which were perpetrated by Caesar Nero. And thus the contents of the entire book have been completely fulfilled by the events which occurred around the time of Nero. For these advocates,

Revelation is now only a book of already fulfilled prophecies. And hence it has no future spiritual value for us Christians. It merely forms a special part of Roman history and/or ancient Church history. But if that is true, then will not Revelation be a quite meaningless book for us Christians today? In view of this, we must investigate and determine as to the exact time in which this book was written so as to prove the error of this rationalistic theory.

I personally believe the book of Revelation was written around 95 to 96 A.D. during the latter half of the reign of Emperor Domitian, the last of the twelve Roman Caesars.

Modern fundamentalist commentators all agree on this time frame. Let us cite some evidence to support this view.

Concerning the view that the book of Revelation was written by the apostle John during the rule of Domitian, there are two strong evidences—both external and internal in nature.* First, the external evidence.

At the outset we may generally say that all writers of the first three centuries, whose statements where found are explicit, agree in ascribing the exile of John and his writing of the Apocalypse (Revelation) to the latter part of the reign of Domitian, the last of the Twelve Caesars, which is therefore to say that it was written in either A.D. 95 or 96.

The first and greatest witness of all is Irenaeus. For

---

*What follows was in large part taken from G. H. Pember, *The Greater Prophecies of the Centuries—Concerning the Church* (London, Hodder and Stoughton, 1909), pp. 429–432.— *Translator* he was a pupil of Polycarp, who himself had been one of John's disciples. Hence Irenaeus is far more likely to have received a true account of John the apostle's closing days than would any other writer whose works have come down to us. So that, when speaking of the strong probability that the name of the Antichrist would be Teitan, Irenaeus gives the following definite testimony concerning John and his apocalyptic writing:

> We will not, however, run the risk of a mistake in this matter, by confidently affirming, that he will have this name; for we know, that, if it were meet that his name should be proclaimed at the present time, it would have been announced by him who saw the Revelation. For it was seen at no distant time, but almost in our own generation, at the end of the reign of Domitian.*

Tertullian, a contemporary of Irenaeus, observed: "How happy a church is that one which Apostles poured out all their doctrines with their blood! Where Peter endures a suffering like to that of his Lord; where Paul has for his crown the same death as John; and the Apostle John, after having been plunged into boiling oil without suffering any harm, was banished to an island."** Here Tertullian informs us of two facts: first, that John was banished; and, secondly, that the place of his exile was an island. In another passage, after mentioning the persecution by Nero, he continues: "Domitian, too, who was somewhat of

---

*Quoted in G. H. Pember, *op. cit.*, p. 429.
**Ibid.*, p. 430.

a Nero in cruelty, had assayed the same thing; but since he was, also, a human being, readily ceased from his attempt, and even restored those whom he had banished."*

Tertullian thus intimates that *banishment* was the usual penalty inflicted upon Christians by Domitian; whereas, as far as extant records go, Nero was accustomed to putting them to death.*

Clement of Alexandria does not mention Domitian by name; but he probably intends him, when he speaks of the "tyrant," after whose death John returned from exile.**

Eusebius, in three passages, states that the banishment of John took place in the reign of Domitian. He also states that the time wherein John received his revelation was in the fourteenth year of the reign of Domitian, which would be 95 A.D.***

Victorinus of Petau, the author of the earliest extant commentary on the Apocalypse itself, explains the words, "Thou must prophesy again concerning many peoples and nations and tongues and kings" (Rev. 10.11 mg.), as follows:

> He spoke thus, because, when John saw this vision he was in the island of Patmos, having been condemned to labour in the mine by Caesar Domitian. There, then, he saw the Apocalypse; and, when, now advanced in years, he was beginning to think that he should obtain his reception into rest through his sufferings. Domitian was slain, and all

---

Ibid., p. 430.
**Note: this would be 96 A.D. *Ibid.*, p. 430.
***Ibid.*, p. 431.

his sentences were cancelled. And thus, John,
after he had been set free from the mine, delivered
this same revelation which he had received from
the Lord.

Again, when discussing the eighth king that is mentioned in the seventeenth chapter of Revelation, Victorinus tells us in his commentary that the sixth was
Domitian, in whose reign the Apocalypse was
written.*

In the fourth century, Jerome testifies that when
John wrote the Apocalypse he was on the island of
Patmos during the fourteenth year of Caesar Domitian (95 A.D.)—the latter being the second Caesar
who persecuted Christians, Nero being the first.

During the first three and a half centuries,
therefore, no writer appears to have suggested any
other date.

But, in the latter half of the fourth century, this
harmony was broken by Epiphanius of Salamis;
whose testimony, however, is absolutely worthless
against that which has been cited, to say nothing of
the fact that it is incredible in itself. For Epiphanius
was one of the most careless and inaccurate of ancient
writers. His remarkable statement is this: that John
returned from exile—at the age of ninety—in the
reign of Claudius. Now, Claudius was assassinated in
A.D. 54; therefore, if John had attained to his
ninetieth year by that time, he must have been some
thirty-three years older than the Lord, and he as well
must have been in his sixty-third year when called to

Ibid., p. 431. Note that Victorinus was martyred in 303 A.D.

be one of the Lord's apostles! It is clear, then, that the Claudian date may be summarily dismissed.*

Hence, the balance of external evidence is overwhelmingly in favor of the Domitianic date. There are many other witnesses whom we have not quoted which would support this view as well.

Just as the external evidence is overwhelming, so the internal evidence is equally strong in the same direction. By internal evidence, we mean the evidence in the text, which proves that Revelation was truly written at the time of Domitian. What follows is that evidence.**

(1) The state of the churches of Asia as described in the seven letters of Revelation chapters 2 and 3 would have required a development of twenty or thirty years beyond what their condition was in Paul's time, and not merely of five or six, which would be all that the Neronic date would allow.

(2) There had already been at least one martyr in Pergamum; and John, in addressing the seven churches of Asia, speaks of himself as having become their companion in tribulation by his banishment to Patmos for the word of God and for the testimony of Jesus Christ. However, the believers in Smyrna were just about to experience a trial of their faith, even to that of death. It is thus evident that a persecution was raging in Asia Minor at the time. And this must have been the persecution of Domitian, since that of Nero

---

Ibid., pp. 431–32.

**Again, for the imformation to follow, the author was much indebted to G. H. Pember, *op. cit.*, pp. 432–33. — *Translator*

does not appear to have extended beyond the immediate neighborhood of Rome; nor does the Neronic persecution seem to have resulted in banishment but simply in capital punishment.

(3) The Balaamites (see Rev. 2.14) had found time to establish themselves in Pergamum.

(4) Jezebel had not only risen to influence in Thyatira, but time for repentance had also been given to her (this according to Rev. 2.20, 21).

The Domitianic date of A.D. 95 or 96 for the writing of the Apocalypse is thus supported both by external and internal evidence.

Due to the fact that Revelation describes itself definitely as a book of prophecy (see 1.3; 22.7, 18, 19), certain Rationalistic teachers have been found to attempt to set the date of writing to the earlier Neronic time, thereby being able to more narrowly apply all the prophecies in the book to the Roman Emperor Nero and the Christians at that time. But we clearly know today that this prophecy had to have been written long *after* the time of Nero. And up to our present day this concluding portion of God's word still remains a prophetic writing concerned with future events yet to come. It is neither allegorical history nor already fulfilled prophecy.

By having demonstated that this book was written at the time of Domitian, the scheme of those Rationalistic teachers to take away this fearful book — it serving as one of the keenest of the swords of God's Spirit — has been defeated.

5 | The Interpretations of "Revelation"

The interpretation of the book of Revelation is a point of contention among commentators. Generally speaking, there are three different schools of interpretation; namely, (1) the Praeterists, (2) the Historical Interpreters, and (3) the Futurists. The Praeterists hold that the whole, or by far the greater part, of the prophecy has been fulfilled in the past struggle between the Church and Rome, with the victory of the Church as the final outcome. Such an interpretation is too abstract and is objected to by orthodox commentators.

The Historical Interpreters hold that the prophecy embraces the whole history of the Church, it showing how the evil forces of the world fight against the Church. This interpretation was very popular during the time of the Reformation and was still strongly advocated in the nineteenth century. Especially with the rise of Napoleon, this view had been recognized as the final interpretation. Among the Protestants, people who hold this view consider the Pope and the Roman

Church to be the Antichrist and the beast. Martin
Luther himself took this view. But the Roman Catholic
commentators took the opposite view and reckoned
that Protestantism was the Antichrist. They even
claimed to have found the number 666 in the name of
Martin Luther. Many of God's people at the end of
the eighteenth and at the beginning of the nineteenth
centuries held that Napoleon fulfilled the personage
mentioned in Revelation 13. And many of the numbers
in the book were arbitrarily taken to be a fixed period
of prophecy; for example, the number of three years
and a half was considered to represent the tribulation
in their own current history.

The Futurists maintain that the greater part of the
prophecy has yet to be fulfilled in the future. Com-
mencing from chapter 4 onwards, not even a letter has
yet been fulfilled. Chapters 2 and 3 speak of the
Church. Only after the Church period has been completed can anything from chapter 4 on be fulfilled.
Chapters 6–19 refer to events that will happen at the
time of the last seven of Daniel's seventy sevens. And
even Daniel's last seven cannot commence until Church
history has been completed. This interpretation is the
most satisfactory one for it coincides most with the prophecies to be found in other passages of the Bible.
Nevertheless, we have no intention to strive after an
opinion! Indeed, may the Lord ever keep us from it.
What we desire is His truth. May His Spirit lead us
into all truths and enable us to understand God's word.

It is unavoidable that there be much argument over
the interpretation of Revelation among these three
schools. But our aim, as we have already made clear,

is to know what *God* wants us to know, not to strive in defense of any human school of opinion. Hence we will not present all the arguments either pro or con. Though these may be welcomed by some people, they are not edifying.

A few words, however, do need to be said to demonstrate that there is fallibility in both the Praeterists and the Historical Interpreters. The Praeterists hold the view of the Rationalistic teachers. No one in the Church of the first few centuries believed it. For it limited the horizon of John to seeing only the Roman persecution of Christians. It reduces the prophecy to allegorical value only, and it merely predicts the defeat of the Romans. The Historical Interpeters, on the other hand, blunt the most solemn warnings of the Holy Bible directed towards the people at the end of this age, so that they cannot know what the wrath of God is to be. Let us therefore be clear as to what the Bible actually teaches.

In 1 Corinthians 10.32 Paul divides mankind into three main categories; namely, Jews, Gentiles, and the Church of God. During the time of the Old Testament there was no Church for it was established by the Lord only in the New Testament period. Since the book of Revelation is the last one in the Bible and by that position it sums up the entire Scriptures, it naturally ought to show us how these three categories of people eventually end up. The Praeterists, though, hold that Revelation relates only to the past history of the struggle of the Church. The Historical Interpreters, too, limit the prophecy to the experience of the Church after the time of John. Both embrace the Church and over-

look the Jews and the Gentiles. Such a view is too lop-
sided and makes the revelation of God in the Bible im-
perfect. For according to their interpretations we would
be left in the dark as to the future end of both the Jews
and the Gentiles. Yet we ought to expect to see in this
last Bible book (1) the course the Church will travel
along on earth and her future glory, (2) the protection
of the Jewish remnant by the Lord through the Great
Tribulation and their receiving the promised blessings
of God as prophesied by the prophets, and (3) the judgment of the Gentiles who sin and disbelieve as well as
the joy of those Gentiles who come to the Lord.

I will not argue which interpretation is right and
which is wrong. There must of course be a true interpretation which agrees with all the prophecies in the
Old and New Testaments and which profits us spiritu-
ally. Where can we find this true interpretation? Any
answer is in the book itself. What this book of Revelation tells us is most trustworthy. We need not spend
very much time in researching the interpretations and
ideas of the different schools. We can even disregard
such terms as the Praeterists or the Futurists. The best
way is to search the Scriptures directly. For I believe
that in the pages of Revelation itself our Lord Jesus
Christ has given us the key to its own interpretation.

The Key to Interpreting "Revelation"

In each book of the Bible there is a key verse, by
which that book can be opened. And hence we would
hope to find the key verse in Revelation so as to give
us the outline of this book too. Where is this verse?

The Lord Jesus himself commanded John to write this book; so let us see how John received the commission: "Write therefore the thing which thou sawest, and the things which are, and the things which shall come to pass hereafter" (1.19). The Lord directed John to write down three main elements: first, the things "which [John] saw"; second, "the things which are"; and third, "the things which shall come to pass hereafter." And John wrote accordingly. At the time he was about to write, he had already seen a vision; therefore, the first thing for him to write was a record of the vision he had just seen. John then continued to set down "the things which are" and concluded with "the things which shall come to pass hereafter." And thus, this one verse of Scripture alludes to the things of the past, the present, and the future.

Three Main Divisions of "Revelation"

Taking this as the key, then, the book of Revelation must be divided into three main parts. With twenty-two chapters in the book, how are the three divisions made? Before we touch upon the first and the second divisions, let us begin by looking at the third. There is a verse in chapter 4 which plainly indicates that the third division commences at that chapter: "After these things," said John, "I saw, and behold, a door opened in heaven, and the first voice that I heard, a voice as of a trumpet speaking with me, one saying, Come up hither, and I will show thee the things which must come to pass hereafter" (4.1). "The things which must come to pass hereafter" must be the things after the first three chapters. Revelation 1.19 indicates that the third division speaks of "the things which shall come to pass hereafter," and the things which John saw from chapter 4 onward are in fact "the things which must come to pass hereafter." It is thus evident that his third division of Revelation commences at chapter 4 (and since the book has only three divisions, the third division must be from chapter 4 through chapter 22). This leaves only the first three chapters for covering the first and the second divisions of the book.

Revelation chapter 1 is concerned with that which John saw. Verse 11 says "What thou seest, write in a book," and in verse 19 John is ordered to "write therefore the things which thou sawest." In between the time of these two verses John saw the vision, which constitutes the things which he saw. The first division of the book is therefore chapter 1. Since we have learned that the whole book by its own description is to be divided into three main divisions, and since we learned also that the first division is chapter 1 and the third division is from chapter 4 to the book's end, it can reasonably be concluded that the second main division of the book must be chapters 2 and 3. In those chapters we will find "the things which are," which are the things concerning the Church.

John lived in the Church age, and therefore the Church is recognized as "the things which are." Chapters 2 and 3 give the prophetic history of the Church from its beginning to its end. It commences with Ephesians forsaking the first love (2.4) and finishes with the Laodiceans being spewed out of the Lord's mouth (3.16). The entire history of the Church is thus being delineated by these seven local churches. Since "the things which shall come to pass hereafter" follow upon "the things which thou sawest, and the things which are," the matters recorded from chapter 4 onward must wait till Church history is concluded before they can be fulfilled. Although today the end is indeed approaching, we must acknowledge that the Church still exists on earth, and hence her time is not yet entirely fulfilled.

This is the teaching of the Scriptures. Revelation 1.19 is in fact the key which unlocks the mystery surrounding the book. And from this verse we have now obtained a true interpretation.

6 | The Message, Style, and Nature of "Revelation"

Although Christ is the theme of this book, it nonetheless records the things at the end of this age. All the things which will come to pass lead to the kingdom of God's covenant. Therefore, this is a book of prophecy.

Such a prophetic nature is clearly stated both at the beginning and at the end of the book (see 1.3; 22.7, 18, 19). The message of this book is to predict the coming events through many visions.

Beginners may be confused by the many symbols in this book. They may deem it too allegorical to be understood. Yet it really is not as difficult as we may think. Though there are numerous symbols, quite a few of them have already been explained in the book itself. Readers should consequently rely on the power of God and read His word with diligence and patience. If patience is needed in seeking after worldly knowledge, how much more it is needed in seeking after spiritual things! There are at least 14 symbols whch have been explained already. And the unexplained ones may not even exceed this number.

(1) Lampstands symbolize the churches (1.20).

(2) Stars stand for the messengers (or angels) of the churches (1.20).

(3) Fire represents the Holy Spirit (4.5).

(4) Horns and eyes also represent the Holy Spirit (5.6).

(5) Incense symbolizes the prayers of the saints (8.3, 4).

(6) Dragon speaks of Satan (12.9).

(7) Frogs stand for unclean spirits (16.13).

(8) Beast typifies king (17.12).

(9) Heads of the beast stand for hills (17.9).

(10) Horns of the beast stand for subordinate kings (17.12).

(11) Waters represent peoples (17.15).

(12) Woman symbolizes the great city (17.18).

(13) Fine linen represents righteousness (19.8).

(14) Wife of the Lamb stands for the city of God (21.9, 10).

Hence do not treat this book as one of symbols. Even though there are more than thirty such symbols, half of them have already been explained. On the average, there is less than one symbol to be found in each chapter, and consequently Revelation cannot in all truth be labeled as a book of symbols. The prophecies in its pages are of two kinds, direct and indirect. The indirect prophecies are embodied in symbols, but as we have already mentioned, these symbols have not been consigned to total darkness since many have already been explained. Thus readers should not be intimidated by these symbols, but should distinguish the unexplained from the explained ones and seek to discover their meanings.

In spite of the adoption of symbols as a style of writing, we must not spiritualize the book *in toto*. Let us keep in mind one important thing, which is, that Revelation is an *opened* book (see 22.10) and not like Daniel which is a *sealed* book (see 12.4). It is called "the Revelation of John" and therefore all the things recorded in it are opened up to be understood. It is written according to facts, and hence it can be taken literally. Inasmuch as the matters recorded at the end of the book which must yet occur are actual miracles such as resurrection, rapture, appearing, and so forth, the things given in the earlier part of the volume must also be actual—in this case, punishments—since this is a book of unity. We are told that there are 119 prophecies in the Old Testament concerning the Lord Jesus. How are these prophecies fulfilled? All of them are literally fulfilled. For example, a virgin giving birth to a son, Bethlehem, the coming up from Egypt, the thirty pieces of silver, and so forth, were all literally fulfilled.

Beyond these symbols, the rest of the book contains the plain sayings of God. We acknowledge that spiritual meanings and teachings are implied. Yet these pictorial parts must be explained literally. For instance, at the opening of the seventh seal, we find that seven angels are ready to blow the trumpets. In the blowing of the seven trumpets there are hail and fire, blood, mountain, sea, stars, moon and sun, and so forth. On the one hand, all these should be taken literally, although we still may derive much spiritual meaning and teaching from them. On the other hand, though, we must not accept merely their spiritual meanings and reject the awfulness of the literal punishments. Here we see the wisdom of God. He hides spiritual meaning in the letter so that those who have learned of God may discover the deeper teaching behind the letter. Yet those ordinary believers may also learn directly from the actual phenomena of future tribulations. The word of God is revealed to babes (Matt. 11.25). How can a baby understand the book of Revelation if it is as deep as some people say? We praise the Lord, that in spite of some difficult passages in Revelation, many more of them are to be literally applied, and therefore babes in Christ may understand the book. We also praise the Lord, because even though Revelation is so plain that ordinary believers may know much of it, the book likewise offers many materials for research to the very best of man's brains. Our God is indeed God!

The character of Revelation is righteous, for from start to finish it manifests the righteousness of God. It is not easy to find in it the grace of God; even towards the Church, it reveals the strict discipline of the Lord. It is, in fact, a book of judgment. In it we see how the Lord judges His Church, the Jews, and the nations. It unveils the Lord Jesus and discloses His judgment.

Due to its character being different from the other books of the New Testament, many people deem Revelation too difficult to understand. Yet it is not really hard to know. The Church has failed, so the Lord can only resort to judgment. What is recorded in chapters 2 and 3 is the foreshadowing of the judgment seat of Christ (2 Cor. 5.10). With the exception of chapters 4 and 5 which narrate matters in transition, the entire record from chapter 6 through chapter 19 belongs to the time of the last seven of Daniel's seventy sevens. Daniel's seventy sevens fall into the dispensation of law. The dispensation of grace is inserted between the sixty-ninth seven and the seventieth seven. As soon as the dispensation of grace concludes, the seventieth seven commences, which still belongs to the dispensation of law. Hence all the things spoken of from chapter 6 through chapter 19 turn back into the dispensation of law. No wonder its character is so righteous.

Due to its righteous and legal character, the book carries within itself much of the Jewish flavor. In this book the Church is presented in somewhat different terms from what the Church is described as in Paul's writings. Although like Paul's writings Revelation is written in Greek, the book nonetheless employs many Hebraisms—such as Abaddan, for example, and so forth. Even the names of our Lord contain Jewish connotations, such as Jehovah God. The Gospel according to Matthew quotes the Old Testament 92 times; the book of Hebrews quotes it about 103 times; but the book of Revelation does so about 285 times! This proves that Revelation shows how God shall return to the Old Testament ground and deal with the nations as well as the Jews accordingly. For let us not forget that salvation is from the Jews. Hence the saints of the Lord should learn to love the Jews and not to reject them. We ought to love the elect of the Lord.

7 | Salvation and Reward

We have now seen that the book of Revelation is a book of righteousness. Yet for us to appreciate its righteous effects, we need to distinguish salvation from reward. The word of God presents a clear distinction between these two. What God has parted, let not men join together. Let us consider this matter carefully and see the contrast between them.

Salvation is that which is *given freely*. It is not earned by means of man's works. For it is God who gives *grace* to us, and not on the basis of our *merit*.

"Ho, every one that thirsteth [points to the sinner], come ye to the waters [points to God's salvation], and he that hath no money [points to works or righteous deeds]; come ye, buy, and eat [means all sinners may believe and be saved]; yea, come, buy wine and milk [means the joy of salvation] without money and without price [points to the fact that there is no need of good deeds, since it does not depend on one's goodness]" (Is. 55.1).

"The *gift* of God" (John 4.10).

"The *free gift* of God is eternal life" (Rom. 6.23).

"By *grace* have ye been saved through *faith*; and that not of yourselves, it is the gift of God; not of works, that no man should glory" (Eph. 2.8, 9).

"Not by works done in righteousness, which we did ourselves, but according to his *mercy* he saved us" (Titus 3.5).

"He that will, let him take the water of life freely" (Rev. 22.17).

Through these verses which have been quoted and many other Scripture passages not quoted, it is proven beyond any doubt that we receive our salvation *freely* and not by our works or righteous acts; we are saved by the *grace* of God, the free gift of God. All we do is to believe. For the work of salvation is wholly done for us by the Lord Jesus. His death on the cross has accomplished our salvation. For us now to be saved and to gain eternal life, there is no need for us to perform more works or to add more merits but simply to *believe* and *receive*. This is because none of our good works is acceptable to God. Throughout the entire New Testament there are about 150 instances of such sayings as these: believe and be saved, believe and have eternal life, believe and be justified. Just as soon as we believe, we are saved, receive eternal life, and are justified. This is all freely given: ". . . the witness is this, that God *gave* unto us eternal life, and this life is in his Son. He that hath the Son hath the life; he that hath not the Son of God hath not the life" (1 John 5.11, 12). All who accept the Lord Jesus as Savior by faith have eternal life according to the word of God.

Truly, "he that *believeth* on the Son hath eternal life" (John 3.36). *Believe* and you have!

Reward, though, is a different matter. It is not something freely received; it must be obtained through *good works*. It is given according to the works of each *saint*. Let us look at the following Scriptures.

"My *reward* is with me, to render to each man *according as his work is*" (Rev. 22.12). Note that this word is spoken to the Church (see v.16).

"Each shall receive his own *reward according to his own labor*" (1 Cor. 3.8).

"Whatsoever ye *do*, work heartily, as *unto* the Lord, and not unto men; knowing that from the Lord ye shall receive the recompense of the inheritance . . . For he that *doeth* wrong shall *receive* again for the wrong that he hath done" (Col. 3.23–25).

"Now to him that *worketh*, the *reward* is not reckoned as of grace" (Rom. 4.4).

There are many more Scriptures which could be quoted, but these above are sufficient to prove that *reward is not freely received*. According to the teaching of the Bible, reward is added to the believer's good works. As insignificant as is a cup of cold water (Matt. 10.42), or as hidden as is the counsel of the heart (1 Cor. 4, 5) or as humble as is one's service (Mark 10.43) or as unknown is the suffering for the Lord's sake (Luke 6.22) – all such deeds or attitudes may still have the opportunity of being rewarded (cf. Luke 6.23).

According to the Bible, the goal which is set before a person is twofold: when we are yet *sinners*, our goal is *salvation*; after we are saved and become *believers* our goal is *reward*. For salvation is provided for sin-

ners, whereas reward is provided for believers. Men
ought to receive salvation first and then pursue after
reward. The perishing should receive salvation; and the
saved should win reward. By reading 1 Corinthians
9.24–27 and Philippians 3.12–14, we can readily see
that some *believers* fail to obtain *reward*. For in these
two passages, Paul is talking about reward and not
about salvation. He well knows that he is saved. In his
other epistles, he frequently expresses himself as one
who has received grace. But in these two passages, he
tells us of what he is seeking after having been saved —
and that is, reward. At this moment he dare not say
for sure that he has achieved the reward, he instead
is still pursuing. Sinners ought to seek for salvation,
while believers ought to seek after reward.

However corrupted a sinner may be, if he is willing to believe the Lord Jesus as Savior, he shall be in-
stantly saved. Once saved and regenerated, he should
seek to develop this new life in him and to serve the
Lord faithfully so that he may obtain the reward. He
is saved through the work of *Christ*; he is rewarded
by his *own* works. He is saved through *faith*; he is
rewarded by *works*. God is willing to save an undeserving sinner, but He will not reward an undeserving
believer. Before anyone believes in the Lord, if he is
willing to acknowledge himself as a sinner, come to
the Lord Jesus and believe in His substitutionary death
on the cross, he is saved and eternal blessing is
guaranteed to him. But according to the Scriptures,
after he is saved he is placed by God on the race course
of life that he may run. If he wins, he shall be rewarded.
If he loses, he will not be rewarded. Yet he *will not*

lose eternal life because of his defeat. For salvation is eternal. Here we find the most balanced teaching, the perfect truth. Unfortunately, many people only know salvation. They are content with merely being saved and do not care about the reward.

How sad that people have mixed up salvation with reward. They reckon salvation is most difficult, requiring their supreme efforts of self-discipline to attain it. But this is not the teaching of the Bible. The Scriptures consider salvation to be that which is most easy to come by, for the Lord Jesus by His own initiative has already accomplished everything for us. But the Scriptures regard reward as that which is somewhat harder to obtain because it depends upon the works which we by *our* initiative accomplish through Christ.

Let us illustrate the matter in this way. Suppose a certain rich man opens a free school. All who attend are free from all charges since this rich man pays for all their expenses. But those who achieve excellence in learning shall receive a special reward. Accordingly, salvation can be likened to entering this free school. All who are willing to come to the Lord Jesus are saved because He himself has paid the cost of salvation. It is very easy to become a student in this free school since it costs nothing. It is enough just to *come*. In like manner, then, salvation is most easy. One need not do anything except *believe*. But for one who is now enrolled as a student, to obtain the reward is not that easy; he must *work* hard. Similarly, it is not so easy for a believer to win the divine reward; he must have *good* works.

Let not any reader think that it is enough to be

saved and not seek the reward as well. To every truly born-again person, the Lord is calling that one to pursue after spiritual excellence—to win the reward. And it should be a natural thing for him to pursue and win. Yet not for his personal benefit, but to gain the Lord's heart and pleasure. For whoever is rewarded by the Lord has delighted His heart. Just as a sinner should be saved, so a believer should be rewarded also. Reward to a believer is as important as salvation to a sinner. If a saint fails to achieve the reward, it does not mean that he has sacrificed his profit, it only indicates that his life is not holy and his labor is not faithful and that he has not manifested the Lord Jesus Christ during his pilgrim days.

Recent teachings have swung towards two extremes. Some reckon salvation to be so difficult that it demands people to do a great deal. Thus they nullify the substitutionary death and the work of redemption of our Lord Jesus. Such teaching puts the entire responsibility on man and overlooks what the Bible says about our being saved by *grace* through faith. Some others think that since all is of grace, then all who believe in the Lord Jesus will not only be saved but also be rewarded with glory and rule in the future with the Lord Jesus. And hence, they lay the entire responsibility on God and neglect what is observed in the Scriptures that some believers—though they be saved—will suffer loss, yet as through fire (1 Cor. 3.15).

Yet there is a most balanced teaching here. Before a sinner believes, the Lord bears His responsibility; after the sinner believes, he must bear the responsibility himself. The work of salvation is totally done by the

Lord for him, so it is enough just to believe. But this matter of reward depends wholly on the believer's works, and therefore to believe alone is not adequate. As a sinner cannot be saved by good works, so a saint cannot be rewarded by only believing. Salvation is based on faith; reward is judged by works. Without faith, there is no salvation; without works, there is no reward. If we carefully study the New Testament, we shall perceive how clearly God separates salvation and reward. Salvation is for sinners, but reward is for saints. Both are divinely ordered: sinners should be saved and saints should be rewarded. Overlooking either of them will incur great loss. Let us therefore not mix salvation and reward together.

What is salvation? It is to not perish but to have eternal life. This is what we all know. Yet this does not decide our positions in glory since those are in fact determined by rewards. What is reward? From the Scriptures we can see that reward is to reign with Christ during the millennial kingdom. Every believer has eternal life; but not every believer will be rewarded by being given the right to reign with Christ. The kingdom of the heavens in the Gospel according to Matthew points to the *heavenly part* of the millennial kingdom—that is to say, it points to our reigning with Christ. Every careful reader of the Gospel can see the difference between eternal life and the kingdom of the heavens. To have eternal life requires only faith, but to gain the kingdom of the heavens demands violence to oneself (see Matt. 11.12). So that to be saved is to have eternal life, while to be rewarded is to enter into the kingdom of the heavens.

Let us all press on towards the goal. May God enable us to forsake everything for His sake in order that we may win His reward. To be saved is something now and instantaneous, because it is recorded in God's word that he who believes has eternal life (see the Gospel according to John). Reward is something in the future, for the Scripture says that when the Lord shall come, "then shall each man have his praise from God" (1 Cor. 4.5). Salvation is now, reward is then. Let us not mix them up, because there is a great difference in the principles which govern salvation and reward. Salvation shows the *grace* of God because He does not recompense us according to our sins but rather saves us who believe in the Lord Jesus. Reward expresses the *righteousness* of God because He recompenses the saints according to their good works. Whoever serves Him faithfully shall receive reward.

Let us never forget that our God is not just gracious, nor is He only righteous; His character bespeaks *both* grace and righteousness. Saving sinners is His act of grace; rewarding saints is his act of righteousness. We earlier observed that the book of Revelation expresses the righteousness of God. Knowing the difference between salvation and reward is essential to our understanding of this book. Otherwise it will be difficult to explain the righteous dealing of God with the saints which is delineated in its pages.

Through John God reveals the word of eternal life. In his Gospel, he shows the way to eternal life. In his epistles, he describes the manifestations of eternal life. But in the book of Revelation, he discloses the judgment of the saved. And hence the last book of the Bible touches very little on the matter of the salvation of believers but rather strongly on the question of their reward. Its pages speak of righteousness, and reward is God's righteous act. By reading chapters 2 and 3 we come to see not the matter of salvation but that of the Christian life, believers' works, and their victory. Such knowledge will help us to grasp hold of not only these two chapters but of the rest of the book as well.

8 | Four Judgments

Having differentiated between reward and salvation, we can now touch upon a related problem — the subject of judgment. Without judgment, how can it be determined who is saved and who is unsaved? Without judgment, how can it be known who will be rewarded and who will suffer loss? The Bible unfolds to us four different kinds of judgment: (1) the Lord Jesus was judged for us on the cross; (2) the believers will be judged as to their works before the judgment seat of Christ; (3) the nations will be judged on earth (Matt. 25.31–46); and (4) God's judgment of the dead (or, of the great white throne) (Rev. 20.11–15). Of these four judgments, one has already passed, but three are coming in the future. All who are willing to believe in the Lord Jesus as their Savior will have their problem of sins forever solved due to the effect of Christ having been judged for sins on the cross. They are therefore saved, they have received eternal life, and they will be judged no more (see John 3.18, Rom. 8.1). They will not be judged for *sins* anymore because the Lord Jesus has suffered for them on the cross.

But although believers will not be judged for sin, the Bible nonetheless indicates that they will still be judged (2 Cor. 5.10; Rom. 14.10-12; Matt. 25.14-30; 1 Cor. 3.10-15; etc.). What judgment is that? Not the judgment as to whether one is saved or perishes, since this issue has already been resolved for the believer by the cross. Moreover, 1 Corinthians 3.15 states that in this judgment there is no danger of perishing. Hence this judgment is that judgment of the works of saints. The judgment of the cross concludes our lives as sinners. The judgment seat of Christ concludes our lives as believers.

Before the judgment seat of Christ we are going to be examined as to our lives lived from the day we first believed in the Lord and onward. Sins which have been confessed will not be brought up. Some believers will have served the Lord faithfully—having suffered much and forsaken all things, having done the will of God without any ulterior motive except to please Him. These people will be rewarded and will reign with Christ in unspeakable glory. How great and good this will be! For the Lord's heart will be pleased, and they will receive glory. Let us seek for it! Some others may have faltered at times, but if they have confessed their sins, they will be washed by the precious blood so that they may renew their pursuit and follow the Lord along the narrow path of the cross. These too shall receive His reward. As to others, however, they may not have sinned, but their works were like wood, hay and stubble since they sought after the approval of men and worked with a double motive. These shall not be rewarded at all but will suffer tremendous loss. And then there will be still others who after being saved will have continued to commit many sins—unconfessed and unrepented of; such people will be punished instead of rewarded. Although their eternal salvation is an unshakable matter, they will nonetheless be severely disciplined by the Lord. Revelation 1–3 discloses the attitude of the Lord Jesus in judging His saints. It is the *prelude* to the judgment seat of Christ.

The third of these four judgments—the judgment of nations—will be determined according to how each nation will have treated the Jews during the Great Tribulation. This judgment will take place at the end of the Tribulation but before the commencement of the millennial kingdom. What is to take place as described in Revelation 16.12–16 and 19.11–21 has reference to this judgment.

The fourth and final judgment is that of the great white throne—that is to say, God's judgment of the dead (see Rev. 20.11–15).

Since the book of Revelation speaks so much of judgment, an awareness of these four judgments to be found in the Scriptures will help us to understand the different judgments spoken of in this final book of the Bible.

9 | The Meanings of the Numerals

"Every scripture inspired of God is also *profitable* for teaching, for reproof, for correction, for instruction which is in righteousness" (2 Tim. 3.16). God uses many numerals in the Bible; to those who love His word these numerals are full of meaning. God's purpose is not to give men wonderful stories to tell, but rather to bless His children. Will it not be a spiritual loss if the children of God overlook the meanings hidden within these numerals in the Bible? To ordinary people, these meanings may look arbitrary; but to the godly, nothing is accidental, for the hand of God is no doubt behind all. Since it pleases God to use many numerals, we should not be so dull as to not find out their meanings. Revelation uses more numerals than is found in the other books of the Bible. In order to rightly divide the word of God, it is imperative that we first understand the Scriptural meaning of these numerals.

The Bible employs the numbers 1 to 7 as the basic roots of all the other biblical numerals. All the other numerals derive their meaning and explanation from these seven basic ones. "7" is a perfect number; and this is known and recognized by many. "8" is not an independent numeral. 7 forms a cycle, and 8 is the beginning of another cycle. All the numerals higher than 7 are formulated from these seven basic numerals by means of adding or multiplying. For example: the numeral "10" comes from the number "5" multiplied by two; the numeral "12" comes from the multiplication of the basic numbers "3" and "4": the numeral "40" is the multiple of the numbers "5" and "2" and "4." Let us now look at a few of these numerals.

The Number "1"

"1" is God's number: "Hear, O Israel: Jehovah our God is *one* Jehovah" (Deut. 6.4); "there is *one* God" (1 Tim. 2.5). 1 represents independence, which admits of no other; it expresses the power of God. 1 implies a sufficiency which needs no other; it shows forth the abundance of God. 1 is the beginning of all numbers; it demonstrates the greatness of God. For He is the source of all things. He is unique. He is the Head of all things. We will receive much help by looking at the way 1 is used in the Bible.

Passover marks the beginning of months; it is to be the first month of the year (Ex. 12.2). This points to the redemption of God. The redemptive work at Calvary heads up all things. That which God created on the first day was light; this is the power of God. The first book of the Bible is Genesis which reveals God's power and glory. All the firstborn of the sons of the Israelites belong to the Lord, for they are holy to the Lord (Ex. 22.29). The first of the firstfruits of the ground must be brought into the house of God, for He should be served first (Ex. 23.19). Unfortunately, many of God's children do not realize that He is one and that therefore they should honor Him as the First. We ought to let Him have the preeminence in all things (Col. 1.18).

1 also speaks of harmony or oneness: "The dream of Pharaoh is one" (Gen. 41.25).

1 also signifies peace: "that they may be one, even as we are" (John 17.11). It shows a relationship.

To sum up, we may say that since 1 is the foundation of all numerals, it is God's number. All things begin at 1; God is the beginning of all things. 1 is the fundamental unit, the summing up of all numbers; and hence God holds all things together in himself. No numeral precedes 1, and thus it represents the absolute God in heaven.

Although this numeral is primarily for God, when it applies to man, it implies an evil sense. It may speak of man's independency, disobedience and rebellion.

The Number "2"

God is three in one and one in three. Within the Trinity, the holy Son is the second Person. Thus, "2" is the number of the Lord Jesus. He is called the second man (1 Cor. 15.47). He has two natures—that of God and man. His works fall into two stages— suffering and glory. In reading Leviticus, we find that a person who sins shall bring two turtle-doves or two

young pigeons to God as his trespass-offering: one is
to be offered as a sin-offering and the other as a burnt-
offering (Lev. 5.7). A sin-offering is offered up for the
sake of sin; a burnt-offering is offered up for the sake
of the person. God forgives sin and accepts the person. This also is two-sided. All this represents the salvation of the Lord Jesus. 2 is likewise the number of
salvation. The second Person in the Godhead—the
Lord Jesus—is the Savior of the world.

2 also speaks of addition, help and fellowship:
"Two are better than one, because they have a good
reward for their labor. For if they fall, the one will
lift up his fellow; but woe to him that is alone when
he falleth, and hath not another to lift him up. Again,
if two lie together, then they have warmth; but how
can one be warm alone? And if a man prevail against
him that is alone, two shall withstand him; and a
threefold cord is not quickly broken" (Eccl. 4.9-12).

2 is the number of testimony as well. The
testimony of two different individuals is true. Please
read Deuteronomy 17.6, 19.15, Matthew 18.16, 2
Corinthians 13.1, and 1 Timothy 5.19. The witness of
God towards men is seen in the Old Testament and
the New. The names of the disciples are given in twos
(Matt. 10.2-4). The disciples went forth to bear
witness two by two. The tablets of the testimony are
two in number. During the Great Tribulation, there
will be two dramatic witnesses (Rev. 11.3). The second Person of the Godhead is the Word of God and
the Faithful Witness (Rev. 19.13; 1.5).

2 has another meaning: it speaks of division, difference and contrast. For instance, during the second

day of creation, God divided the waters from the waters. The animals entered the ark in pairs (Gen. 6.19,20). A woman who bore a maid-child would be unclean for two weeks, doubling the days for bearing a male-child (Lev. 12.5).

2 has still another meaning: it is the number of production. 2 is the first number after 1 is added on; it is therefore not a complete number. More numbers may be added onto it to make it perfect. The Holy Father and the Holy Son are not complete without adding the Holy Spirit to the Trinity. The husband and wife are joined in one, but in God's eyes the family is not complete till children are added.

The Number "3"

"3" is the number of personal completeness. It is the number of the Godhead, it standing for the triune God. It is formed by 1 plus 1 plus 1. But if the 1's are multiplied, the result is still 1. So that God is 3 in 1 and 1 in 3. In geometry two lines do not make a cube. Hence 2 is an incomplete number while 3 is the first complete number. It therefore represents God. A complete man is formed with spirit, soul and body. A complete family is composed of father, mother and children. A complete faith consists of knowledge, works and experience.

3 is also a number of resurrection. The Lord Jesus is resurrected on the third day. The earth came out of the water on the third day. A person is born again through the preaching of the gospel which comes not in word only but also in power and in the Holy Spirit

(1 Thess. 1.5). Jonah was in the belly of the fish for three days. The restoration of the nation of Israel is also connected with the numeral 3 (Hosea 6.1,2).

This number 3 is frequently related to God; such as when people are baptized into the name of the Father and of the Son and of the Holy Spirit (Matt. 28.19). The benediction of the apostle Paul is also couched in the Triune formula of 3 in 1 (2 Cor. 13.14). The Lord Jesus was tempted three times; and He prayed three times in the garden of Gethsemane. Peter denied the Lord three times; he was asked three times by the Lord: "Lovest thou me?"; and three times he was told, "Feed my sheep" (John 21.15–17). "There are three who bear witness" to the Son (1 John 5.8). In praising God, the seraphim cried one to another: "Holy, holy, holy" (Is. 6.3). The four living creatures are also found saying, "Holy, holy, holy" (Rev. 4.8). The largest piece of furniture in the tabernacle is the altar, which is capable of containing all the rest of the tabernacle furniture. The altar stands for the cross which satisfies the righteousness of God. It is three cubits tall, signifying that the righteousness of the cross has reached the standard of God. When God judged men's sin in Christ, the heaven and earth were darkened for three hours. According to Hebrews 9.23–28, the Lord Jesus appears three times: the first time He appeared to put away sin (v.26); the second time He appears before the face of God to intercede for us (v.24); and the third time He shall appear to them who wait for Him to the redemption of their body (v.28).

The Number "4"

"4" is the number of the world. God apportions the world dominion to four kingdoms: Babylon, Medo-Persia, Greece and Rome. The materials representing world power in Nebuchadnezzar's image are gold, silver, brass and iron (Dan. 2). The world kingdoms in God's eyes are like four beasts (Dan. 7). 4 as the number of the world may also be seen in this number's relationships with the world. The world has four seasons: spring, summer, fall and winter. It has four corners: east, west, south and north (Num. 2). It has four basic elements: earth, air, water and fire. It has four winds (Rev. 7.1). The river which flowed out of the earth's paradise — the garden of Eden — was parted and became four heads (Gen. 2.10-14). The living creatures which represent the created world are four in number (Rev. 4.6). In Ezekiel we are told that the cherubim, which are the same as the living creatures, have four faces: that of the lion, ox, man, and eagle; and they have also four wings (ch. 1). Mankind on earth is described in a foursome: peoples, multitudes, nations, and tongues (Rev. 17.15). The heart conditions of men, according to the parable of the sower as spoken by the Lord Jesus, are of four kinds (Matt. 13.3-9, 18-23). The tribulations which come as judgment upon the world are also four in number: war, famine, pestilence and earthquake (Matt. 24.6,7 AV; cf. Luke 21). Those which bear witness to the Lord Jesus are the four Gospels which reveal the four aspects of Christ. At the height of men's sin, the four soldiers divided among themselves the garments of the Lord Jesus (John 19.23). The altar set up for men is "foursquare" with four horns (Ex. 27.1,2). The fourth of the Ten Commandments is the first of the remaining ones that touch upon the things of the world (Ex. 20). The fourth clause in the so-called Lord's Prayer is also that which commences to deal with matters pertaining to this earth (Matt. 6.9–13). The things God created on the fourth day were to rule over the days and nights on earth. The fourth book of the Bible, Numbers, relates the experience of the wilderness which is a type of the world.

4 comes from 3 plus 1; and 3 is the foundation of 4. As 3 represents God, so 4 represents the created ones who depend on the Creator. 4 is the first number which allows of simple division, even as 2 is the number which divides it. It is therefore the symbol of weakness. The created have really nothing of which to boast.

The Number "5"

"5" has several meanings which are all closely related. 5 is an incomplete number and the number of man's responsibility before God. Owing to its incompleteness, it suggests responsibility. 5 is 4 plus 1. 4 represents the created man, while 1 represents the independent God. So that 5 is man before God. Accordingly, it on the one hand stands for God giving grace to man; it on the other hand represents man bearing responsibility before God. Upon receiving

God's grace, man is naturally held responsible to God.

The incompleteness of the numeral 5 can easily be seen. Man's five fingers and five toes are but half the total fingers and toes. On the fifth day God created the living creatures of the sea, but there was yet no life on earth. At the opening of the fifth seal, how anxious are the martyrs of the ages because they have not yet received their crowns (Rev. 6.7–11). The wrath of the fifth bowl is poured on the throne of the beast, but the power of the beast still waits to be completely destroyed (Rev. 16.10,11). Of the virgins, five are wise and five are foolish (Matt. 25.2); so at the coming of the Lord Jesus Christ not all the saved are ready.

5 also speaks of man's responsibility through grace. The consecration of Aaron and his sons (Lev. 8) and the cleansing of the leper (Lev. 14) are full of meaning. Blood is applied on the tip of the right ear, the thumb of the right hand, and the big toe of the right foot. Ear, thumb and toe are all related to the number 5. Ear is one of the five organs; thumb is one of the five fingers, and big toe is one of the five toes. These three represent the whole person — how he must use his ear to listen to God's word, his hand to do God's work, and his foot to walk in God's path. Together they express man's responsibility before God. He first receives grace through the application of the precious blood. Then having been cleansed by the precious blood, his whole being is responsible before God to walk worthy of the grace of his calling.

4 is a weak number; without adding one more to it so as to become 5, it is not able to bear any responsibility. Take the hand illustration: though the four fingers are quite lively, yet without adding the thumb, the hand is not able to take up responsibility. The Lord Jesus uses five loaves to feed the five thousand hungry (Matt. 14.17); this expresses the Lord's grace. David chooses five smooth stones to overcome Goliath (1 Sam. 17.40); this manifests man's responsibility. The fifth book of the Bible, Deuteronomy, relates how God gives grace and how people are responsible afterwards. The fifth kingdom of the world will be the kingdom of the Lord Jesus Christ (Dan. 2.35,44; Rev. 11.15). All who desire to enter His kingdom and to reign with Christ have tremendous responsibility! Matthew 5–7 lays down the conditions. Deuteronomy, the fifth book of the Bible, speaks also of how the people must behave after entering the promised land, which is a type of the kingdom of our Lord Jesus.

Pentecost is the fiftieth day after Passover. It typifies the coming of the Holy Spirit and the forming of the Church with Jews and Gentiles (see Lev. 23.15–21, where the two loaves represent the Church which is composed of both the Jews and the Gentiles). People receive the Holy Spirit by grace; but whoever lies to the Holy Spirit shall receive severe judgment, and this is responsibility. The book of Leviticus uses five offerings to represent the sacrifice of the Lord Jesus once and for all, to which men are held responsible. The curtains of the tabernacle are 5 in number coupled together one to another, and the pillars of the screen are 5 in number. 5 is the number used frequently in the measurement of the tabernacle.

The Number "6"

"6" is the number of the devil. It is also the number of man because man has sinned by listening to the word of the devil, and hence he is joined with the devil. Before dawn, the darkness of the night seems to deepen; likewise, the number 6 before the complete number 7 is also at its worst. 6 is a number which can be divided; it is therefore a weak number. Men as well as the devil are always weak. That number is lower than the number 7; consequently, men and the devil can never overcome God. May people always realize that their number is 6.

Man was created on the sixth day (Gen. 1). Men should work for six days in a week (Ex. 23.12). A Hebrew serves as slave for only six years (Deut. 15.12). The land of Canaan is to be cultivated successively for six years (Lev. 25.3). Human history is altogether about six thousand years. Moses waited in the mountain for six days before God appeared to him (Ex. 24.15–18). The throne of Solomon has six steps to ascend (1 Kings 10.19). The hours of the day may be divided by 6. Athaliah usurped the throne for six years (2 Kings 11.3). In Genesis 4.16–24, we read that the descendants of Cain are recorded up to the sixth generation. The sixth letter to the Church mentions the hour of trial upon the whole earth (Rev. 3.10). The sixth seal reveals the wrath of the Lamb upon mankind (6.12ff.). The sixth trumpet predicts the killing of one third of the world population (9.13ff.). The sixth bowl prepares the way for the kings of the world—under the instigation of the unclean spirits—to war against Christ (16.12ff.). The human name of the incarnated Word is Jesus, which in the Greek original is composed of six letters. Six times the Lord Jesus was attacked as demon possessed; how the natural man is always ready to attack our most holy Lord.

When man under the hand of Satan opposes God, his number is frequently connected with the number 6. Goliath is the first example mentioned: his height was six cubits and a span, and his spear's head weighed six hundred shekels of iron (1 Sam. 17.4,7). The golden image of Nebuchadnezzar is the second example: its height was sixty cubits, and its breadth was six cubits (Dan. 3.1–3). The future Antichrist is the third example: his number will be 666 (Rev. 13.18). One comforting thought should be mentioned here: no matter whatever men or the devil may do, the number is only 6, whereas the number of our God is 7; as a consequence, men and devils can never measure up to God.

The Number "7"

"7" is the number of perfection. It is formed by adding 3 to 4. 4 represents man and 3 represents God. And hence it is the joining of God and man. It is therefore perfect. (Note, however, that 7 is also a number of temporary perfection; "12" is the number for permanent perfection.) It often alludes to the proximity of God and man, to the joining of the created to the Creator.

There are numerous examples of 7 as a symbol of perfection. The first seven appears as the Sabbath of God, a holy day in which God rested (Gen. 2.1-3)—a perfect rest. Enoch is the seventh from Adam (Jude 14)—a perfect man. After Noah entered the ark, God gave seven days of grace (Gen. 7.4)—a perfect waiting. Jacob served Laban for Rachael seven years (Gen. 29.20)—a perfect service. Egypt had seven years of abundance and seven years of famine (Gen 41)—perfect grace and punishment. The golden lampstand in the holy place had seven branches (Ex. 25.37)—a perfect association. Aaron and his sons must wear the holy garments for seven days (29.29,35)—perfect holiness. If anyone should sin, the priest must dip his finger in the blood and sprinkle the blood seven times in the presence of the Lord before the veil of the sanctuary for that person (Lev. 4.6)—a perfect cleansing. Aaron and his sons must abide in the tabernacle for seven days (Lev. 8.35)—a perfect abiding. The blood of the Day of Atonement must be sprinkled seven times before the mercy seat (Lev. 16.14)—a perfect redemption. During the feast of unleavened bread, an offering made by fire must be offered for seven days (Lev. 23.8)—a perfect consecration. The feast of the tabernacles was kept for seven days (Lev. 23.42)—perfect glory. In the seventh year the land was not to be sown (Lev. 25.4)—a perfect rest. In fighting against Jericho, seven priests blew seven trumpets as the people of Israel marched around the city for seven days before the city fell (Joshua 6)—perfect obedience and perfect victory. Solomon built the temple in seven years and held the feast of dedication for seven days (1 Kings 6.38; 8.65,66)—a perfect work and perfect worship. Naaman bathed in the river Jordan seven times (2 Kings 5.14)—perfect trust. Job had seven sons (Job 1.2)—a perfect blessing. Job's friends sat on the ground and bemoaned silently for Job seven days and seven nights (Job 2.13)—perfect sorrow. Later they offered seven bullocks and seven rams as a burnt-offering (Job 42.8)—a perfect repentance. The Lord Jesus spoke seven words on the cross—expressions of perfect grace. Seven deacons served the tables (Acts 6.3)—perfect labor.

The Old Testament uses the seven feasts of the children of Israel to typify the temporary way God will treat the world. The New Testament uses seven parables to reveal the conditions of the mysteries of the kingdom of the heavens (Matt. 13). The book of Revelation records seven letters to foretell the conditions of the Church at various periods (Rev. 2 and 3). All these, however, are for a time and may soon pass away.

In the book of Revelation we can notice many sevens. A brother has observed that Revelation is a book of "sevens": it has seven visions, seven words of praising the Lord God and the Lamb, seven Spirits before the throne of God, seven golden lampstands, seven lamps of fire, the Lamb having seven horns and seven eyes, seven angels blowing seven trumpets, seven thunders, seven heads of the beast, seven bowls of God's seven plagues, and seven mountains representing seven kings. Altogether the book uses "7" 56 times. Since it discloses how God will treat men at the final age, this number 7 stands for dispensational perfection, which is temporary perfection.

The Number "8"

"8" is the number of resurrection. The Lord Jesus was resurrected from the dead on the first day of the week, which is the eighth day. Noah is the eighth person preserved by God (2 Peter 2.5) and he has a family of eight (1 Peter 3.20). They came out of the ark (the flood representing death) and multiplied and filled the new earth. God commanded Abraham to circumcise all the male children on the eighth day of birth (Gen. 17.11–14). The meaning of circumcision is the "putting off of the body of the flesh" (Col. 2.11). This agrees with "we are [God's] workmanship, created in Christ Jesus" (Eph. 2.10). David was the eighth son of Jesse (1 Sam. 16.10,11), and he established the new Israel. The leper was cleansed on the eighth day (Lev. 14.10,23) and hence he was declared to be a new person. The sheaf of the firstfruits was waved before the Lord on the eighth day—that is to say, "on the morrow after the sabbath" (Lev. 23.11). Fifty days later was the feast of Pentecost (v.16), which signifies the coming of the Holy Spirit and the commencement of the new age. The feast of the tabernacles lasted for seven days, and on the eighth day there was a holy convocation (v.36); inasmuch as the feast typifies the millennial kingdom, the holy convocation speaks of the new rest after the millennial kingdom. The priests were also consecrated for seven days, and on the eighth day they began their new office (Lev. 9.1). In the eighth year, the children of Israel sowed the land again (Lev. 25.22). Psalm 8 speaks of the kingdom of the Lord (cf. Heb. 2.5–9). The transfiguration of our Lord Jesus happened on the eighth day (Luke 9.28), which event foretells His power and His appearing (2 Peter 1.16–18). The name "Jesus" in Greek is composed of six letters, all of them carrying various numerical values respectively. By adding these numerical values, the total number in the Greek name for "Jesus" comes to 888. The disciples gathered to break bread on the first day of the week, which is the eighth day (Act. 20.7); this is a new day for gathering. On the eighth day, also, the disciples gave their offering (1 Cor. 16.1,2), which action was not according to the statute of the Old Covenant. The eighth head of the beast will be the seventh head resuscitated (Rev. 17.11). The unclean spirits came back with seven other spirits more evil than itself; so eight of them re-entered into the heart of the one who did not receive the Lord Jesus (Matt. 12.43,45). Three of the ten horns on the fourth beast mentioned in Daniel were destroyed, but another horn, a little one, came up as the eighth one, who again spoke blasphemously (see Dan. 7).

The Number "10"

"10" is the number of world perfection; it is also the multiplication of the basic number "5" by 2, and therefore it represents the total responsibility of men before God. A normal person has ten fingers and ten toes for work and for walking. For human rebellion, God punished the Egyptians with ten plagues. At the height of the power of the nations there will be ten kingdoms, which are suggested by the ten toes and ten horns (Dan. 2, 7.7; Rev. 17.12). There are ten commandments given to Israel as their responsibility before God. Ephraim represented the ten tribes of the nation of Israel and was therefore directly responsible to God; Ephraim was not included in Judah. After His resurrection, Christ appeared ten times. How great was the responsibility of those who knew His resurrection!

The church in Smyrna shall have tribulation ten days (Rev. 2.10). The disciples prayed for ten days before they were baptized in the Holy Spirit (Acts 1). The final conditions of the Christians are represented in the parable of the ten virgins (Matt. 25.1,2); among whom five are wise and five foolish but all are held responsible at the arrival of the bridegroom. The woman with ten pieces of silver (Luke 15.8–10) shows that the whole world (at the time of speaking this may have represented only the children of Israel) belongs to God. The ten servants received ten pounds to trade with until the Lord returned (Luke 19.13). They were not to be careless about that which they received. The first servant earned ten pounds, so he was rewarded with ten cities. God required the children of Israel to give one tenth; this proves the greatness of the Lord since everything was given to them by Him. Ten is a number used extensively in the tabernacle, the temple of Solomon, and the temple mentioned in Ezekiel; for all are in this world (Ex. 26.27; 1 Kings 6; Ez. 40).

The Number "12"

"12" is the number of permanency. As the basic number "7" represents temporary or dispensational perfection, so 12 speaks of permanent perfection. 7 is made up of the basic number "4" (man) added to the basic number "3" (God)—the joining together of the created with the Creator. 12 is 4 multiplied by 3, and therefore it is the created being united with the Creator. 7 represents the coming together of man and God, whereas 12 speaks of how God gives grace to man so that the created can be united to the Creator. The former number signifies the contact of the created with the Creator; it is perfect, yet it is only temporary; but the latter number shows forth the union of the created with the Creator, so that it is not only perfect but also permanent. Let us understand that both 7 and 12 come from the two numerals 4 and 3; except that 7 is the *adding* of these two numerals together, whereas 12 is the *multiplying* of them together. To add is to put together, to multiply is to unite in one. Hence the meaning of multiplication is deeper than that of addition. Here we see the importance of being united with God.

Other instances of the biblical use of the number 12 can be seen in the following. A year has twelve months. The nation of Israel was composed of twelve tribes. Mounted on the breastplate of the high priest were twelve precious stones (Ex. 28.21). On the golden table of shewbread were placed twelve loaves of bread (Lev. 24.5,6). Elim had twelve springs (Ex. 15.27). There were twelve men sent to spy out the land (Num. 13). Joshua put twelve stones into the river Jordan (Josh. 4.9). Elijah used twelve stones with which to build an altar (1 Kings 18.31,32). The Lord Jesus went to Jerusalem at twelve years of age (Luke 2.42). He chose twelve apostles and promised them the right to sit on twelve thrones to judge the twelve tribes of Israel (Matt. 19.28). He healed the woman who had had an issue of blood for twelve years (Luke 8.43,44). He raised the twelve-year-old daughter of Jairus from the dead (Luke 8.42,54,55). The leftovers from the five loaves and two fishes after feeding the five thousand were twelve basketsful (Matt. 14.20). The Lord could have, had He done so, asked the Father to send twelve legions of angels to rescue Him (Matt. 26.53).

In reading the book of Revelation, we find that the number 12 is used more frequently than in any other book. There will be twelve stars making up the crown on the woman's head (Rev. 12.1). The New Jerusalem will have twelve gates made of twelve pearls (21.21). At these gates there will be twelve angels (v.12), and the names written above the gates are to be the names of the twelve tribes of Israel (v.12). The city wall will have twelve foundations with the names of the twelve apostles on them (v.14). The tree of life is to bear twelve different fruits (22.2). In the light of all this, we need to notice that in the eternal kingdom of the new heaven and the new earth, all the numbers are to be twelve, none will be seven. In the first half of the book of Revelation, 7 is frequently the number used because it speaks of the conditions of this temporary age. But for the eternal kingdom, 12 is the number used. It is thus proven beyond doubt that 7 is representative of temporary perfection whereas 12 is representative of permanent perfection.

Additional Insights Regarding the Numbers in the Bible

In the Bible can be found many other numerals, all of which are full of meaning; but for our purpose, what we have just now explained should be quite sufficient. Let us look, though, at some adjoining numbers and see the wonderful meanings implied. As we have come to recognize, the basic numbers from 1 to 7 form a cycle in the Bible; and their order is quite meaningful. All the other numerals in the Bible emerge from the adding or multiplying of these seven numbers, and consequently these seven numbers serve as the radicals for all other numerals. Each of these numbers has its own meaning as well as its *good* or *bad* application. For example, if the number 1 has reference to God, it is looked upon as being good; but if it should have reference to man, it is perceived as being bad.

The numerals 1, 2, and 3 express the satisfaction of God—the Father, the Son, and the Holy Spirit. God must precede all numbers; He has the preeminence in all things; otherwise we would see chaos.

4 is the symbol of the created. According to the

Scriptures, 4 is divided into 3 and 1. 4 is the first number after 3. If 3 represents God, 4 signifies that which comes out of God—the created. It also reflects the relationship between the created and the Creator. The created comes from the Creator. How sad that people do not realize or acknowledge that. Apart from the Creator and the created, there is nothing else in the universe. Hence 3 plus 4 form a perfect number.

5, 6, and 7 use 4 as its basic root. 1, 2, and 3 are the first three numbers in the numeral 7; they represent the greatness of the Creator. 4 stands in the midst of the numeral 7; it represents the created. 5, 6, and 7 are the last three numbers in the numeral 7, and therefore they stand for the conditions of the created. 5 is 4 plus 1; 6 is 4 plus 2; and 7 is 4 plus 3. 3 is the number of God, and 4 is the number of man. The relationship of God's number and man's number is limited to 7, and so 7 is a perfect number.

5 is 4 plus 1; it shows how the created (4) is contradictory to the Creator (1). However, it is 4 plus 1, and hence the number 5 speaks of how the created stands before the Creator. It reflects a sense of responsibility. Although the Creator has grace, the world is not thereby freed from responsibility. Any numeral with multiples of the number 5 in it always carries the meaning of responsibility, such numerals for instance as 10, 40, etc.

6 is 4 plus 2; such a number signifies how inadequate and full of strife (2) is the created (4). It also indicates how the created (4) receives help and deliverance (2). 6, therefore, shows forth the actual condition of the fallen world.

7 is 4 plus 3; this number indicates the acceptance of the created (4) by the Creator (3). 7 is a perfect number.

If we study the numerals in the Bible and what they represent, we will not fail to praise God for His wisdom and to marvel at His thought and instruction! By knowing the general concept of these numbers, we will add new meaning to our study of the book of Revelation.

10 | The Year-Day Theory

Recently the study of prophecy had earned for itself a bad reputation among believers because of the so-called year-day theory. According to this theory, many numbers of days in the Scriptures are computed as though a day were a year, thus fostering predictions as to the precise date for the second coming of the Lord Jesus Christ — an exercise of the mind which is plainly contradictory to the Lord's announcement: for no one knows the date of His return, not even Jesus himself. Then, too, some commentators on Revelation have twisted God's word in ways that are meant to fit in with this year-day theory. We have no intention to argue about this theory; we only desire to point out a right understanding of the "days" that are mentioned in the Bible.

The advocates of the year-day theory base their conception on Numbers 14.34 and Ezekiel 4.6. Let us first examine Numbers: "After the number of the days in which ye spied out the land, even forty days, for every day a year, shall ye bear your iniquities, even forty years, and ye shall know my alienation." Here we are told that due to their unbelief, the children of Israel were disciplined by God for forty years, a year for every day they had spied out the land. But this does not apply equally to other "days" mentioned in Scripture, and certainly not to the "days" found in Revelation. As to Ezekiel: "And again, when thou hast accomplished these, thou shalt lie on thy right side, and shalt bear the iniquity of the house of Judah: forty days, each day for a year, have I appointed it unto thee." Here we see that God commanded Ezekiel to lie down in a certain position as a response to the iniquity of Judah. This has nothing to do with the other "days" found in the Bible.

Let us look at a few more passages.

(1) "And yet seven days, and I will cause it to rain upon the earth forty days and forty nights" (Gen. 7.4). Did God wait for seven years and then have the rain fall for forty years? No, for the record goes on to explain as follows: "And it came to pass after the seven days, that the waters of the flood were upon the earth. . . . And the rain was upon the earth forty days and forty nights" (vv.10,12). Here, a day is not a year.

(2) "Joseph said unto him, This is the interpretation of it: the three branches are three days; within yet three days shall Pharaoh lift up thy head" (Gen. 40.12,13). Was it that after three years the chief butler was released from prison? Not at all: "And it came to pass the third day . . . [that] he restored the chief butler unto his butlership again" (vv.20,21).

(3) "Then said Jehovah unto Moses, Behold, I will rain bread from heaven for you; and the people shall go out and gather a day's portion every day . . . And it shall come to pass on the sixth day . . . [that] it shall be twice as much as they gather daily" (Ex. 16.4,5). The children of Israel went out to gather manna every day, not once a year.

(4) God gave meat to the children of Israel to eat for "a whole month" (Num. 11.19, 20). They did not eat meat for thirty years.

(5) "Within three days ye are to cross this Jordan" (Joshua 1.11). What actually happened afterwards? Did the children of Israel cross over Jordan after three years? No, they crossed after three days.

(6) "For as Jonah was three days and three nights in the belly of the whale; so shall the Son of man be three days and three nights in the heart of the earth" (Matt. 12.40). Was the Lord Jesus in the heart of the earth for three years? We know from the biblical record that He was there for only three days and three nights.

From this evidence, therefore, we can easily conclude that the year-day theory is erroneous. If some of the "days" appearing in the book of Revelation are to be taken as years, then the rest of the "days" found therein should also be treated as years. And in that case, the three and a half years of the Great Tribulation would have to be calculated as a thousand two hundred and sixty years; and the millennial kingdom would have to be extended out to three hundred and sixty thousand years. Obviously, we know that such calculations as these cannot be true.

May we therefore trust the Holy Spirit to guide us correctly as we read the word of God. Let us not seize upon strange ideas like this. Even though the Bible is most wonderful, it is not to be explained in any quaint or bizarre way. We ought to learn to be more obedient to God in our thought. And then we will not be likely to misinterpret His word.

11 | The Writings of Peter, Paul, and John

The writer of the Revelation is the apostle John. There are many evidences to support this conclusion, though we will not discuss them here. There is one thing, however, which we ought to recognize about the characteristic of John's writing. In what respect are his New Testament writings different from those of Paul and Peter? We know that both Peter and Paul were chosen by the Lord to establish the Church. In his Gospel and in his Epistles, John seldom touches upon the truth of the Church; and yet, in the first and second main division of the book of Revelation we find that the Lord commanded him to write to seven local churches. For us to understand the condition and status of the Church as revealed in the first three chapters of Revelation, we need to examine carefully the difference as well as the relationship between his writings and the writings of Peter and Paul.

It is evident in the Scriptures that Peter is a minister to the Circumcision while Paul is a minister to the Uncircumcision. Peter and the eleven apostles live in Jerusalem and do the work of the Lord by gathering the lost sheep of *Israel* to form the Church. Paul is called by the Lord and then given revelation concerning the truth of the Church by calling the *nations* (Col. 1.24ff.) to Christ through the preaching of the gospel. He is the one to lay the foundation. The work of Peter is more restricted to the Jews; he leads us to commence our heavenly pilgrimage for the (lost) inheritance of Israel reserved for us in heaven. The work of Paul is far more extended to the Gentiles; he shows us our heavenly position and possession in Christ. These are the important truths of the New Testament time because God deals with people according to special dispensation.

The work of John, though, is quite different. He does not teach dispensational truth. In his Gospel, he makes no mention of the ascension of Christ; in his Epistles, he does not point out the heavenly position of the saints. He concentrates instead on the Lord Jesus as the Word becoming flesh, a coming from heaven to earth. He looks upon the Lord Jesus as the eternal life. And hence, in his Gospel, John announces the birth of that eternal life; and furthermore, in his Epistles, he explains the nature of this eternal life.

The year 70 A.D. — when Jerusalem was destroyed — is a transitional time for dispensational truth. The Jewish Church formed on the day of Pentecost came to an end (actually, it had already been ended, only this was publicly made manifest then). The truths of Christ and of Judaism are not totally separated. Christians ought now to go out of the camp of Judaism. The Church which Peter established among the Jews has failed; Christ is no longer ruling over it.

As this became true among the Jews, so this is also true among the Gentiles: the churches which the Lord used Paul to establish among the nations have also fallen away so that they are unable to inherit the lost inheritance of Israel: "They all seek their own," wrote Paul, "not the things of Jesus Christ" (Phil. 2.21); "All that are in Asia [including the church in Ephesus] turned away from me" (2 Tim. 1.15). Those who knew the Church truth best were unable to stand firm in faith! Indeed, apostasy has already begun and the mystery of lawlessness has also germinated.

The works of Peter and Paul suffer dispensational change, but the work of John transcends the dispensational framework. He shows forth the Lord Jesus as the eternal life, and eternal life, as we know, is unchanging. Although dispensations may change and human events may encounter change, the eternal life found in the Lord Jesus or in the believers never changes. Though the Church may be spewed out of the Lord's mouth, the Lord himself remains the same. The work of John follows upon the works of Peter and Paul, and it supplies their lack. Time-wise, he joins together the first and the second comings of Christ, and his work covers the duration. He preaches on the person of Christ and the eternal life.

In spite of the fact that the outward dispensation has changed and been corrupted, the eternal life remains unchanged. This we see in the last two chapters of John's Gospel. Chapter 20 represents what is to transpire from the resurrection of Christ to His acceptance by the Jewish remnant in the last day. Thomas, looking at the pierced Savior, serves as a type of this. And chapter 21 typifies the gathering in the millennial kingdom. At the end of chapter 21 we are shown the specific works assigned to John and Peter (Paul's Church truth is all heavenly, so it is not mentioned here). The flock of Christ as of Israel is committed to Peter; but he will die before John, and hence his work is not permanent but has an ending. Later on, in fact, Peter's work *is* terminated, the Church of the Circumcision is left without a shepherd, and not long afterwards Jerusalem is destroyed. Thus this work comes to a complete end.

But then we may recall that Peter asks the Lord Jesus about the work of John. It is rather amazing that our Lord does not mention John's death but only calls Peter to follow Him (to die and to finish the work). He hints, though, that the work of John may continue on till His return. Though John himself will die, his work does not die. His writings will continue to have their impact until the second coming of the Lord.

The works of these three apostles are therefore most important for us to grasp. The work of John spans the two comings of Christ. Now we may see the Church truth. Peter tells us of the failure of the Jewish Church, and Paul, of the failure of the Gentile Church. John, being a minister neither to the Circumcision nor to the Uncircumcision, is not entrusted with dispensational truth; and hence he makes no mention of the change in the Jewish or the Gentile Church. What he records in Revelation is instead the actual conditions of the churches at that time. He does not trace the history of the Church to its current state; he merely reports the various conditions of the churches in failure and also the pertinent judgments of the Lord pronounced upon them. After the works of Peter and Paul have ended, John continues on with their works: he simply narrates the fallen condition of the churches at his time.

The churches John writes about, aside from Revelation 22.17, are quite different from those written about by Paul. The testimony of John is to view every local assembly by itself. Some lampstands have the danger of being removed. The churches he sees are by and large already fallen and are now judged by Christ. The Church has failed! The Gentiles who by faith are grafted into the olive tree do not abide in the mercy of God. Paul teaches the church in Ephesus much on Church truth, but now she has left her first love and her lampstand will soon be removed! Just as Israel was cut off by God in the past, so the Church will now also be cut off. Just as God was formerly patient with Israel, so He is now patient towards the Church today. Yet the Church, like Israel, is not able to testify for God in the world.

The Church has already been corrupted and defeated, no matter how long the dispensation is to be extended; at the time of the writing of Revelation God has at least begun to be dissatisfied with His Church. He is going to take a new departure. Hence the Holy Spirit expresses on the one hand God's dissatisfaction with the Church and on the other hand Christ's obtaining of the kingdom. Hereafter the kingdom will be the objective. The Lord uses the seven churches existing in those days to represent the Church in order to let people know that He is dissatisfied with her and that the end is coming. Should the Lord delay His return, then these seven local churches in their current condition will be sufficient to represent and to delineate the entire external history of the Church on earth. And in so doing, the Lord reveals that the end is come and that He can return at any time. This is the wisdom of the Holy Spirit! And as the Lord does indeed delay His coming again, the second and third chapters of Revelation can and do in fact serve to disclose the conditions of the entire Church from the time of John up to the very day before the return of the Lord.

We ought to recognize the fact that during the time of Peter and Paul, the Church had already fallen. Such knowledge will help us in understanding the teaching concerning the Church to be found in the first three chapters of Revelation. In view of the failure of the Church, we ought to see here that Christ is not acting in the capacity of an *intercessory* priest but rather in that of a *judging* priest. We are thus instructed that there is not a perfect Church, and hence we can be delivered from entertaining any false hope about the Church. We will then know what kind of attitude we ought to take towards the Church. For God alone is true, but every man is a liar (cf. Rom. 3.4a).

We have just pointed out the relationship of the Church conditions—as revealed in the first three chapters of Revelation—with the other teachings on the Church.

We must now consider the next division of the book. The third division of Revelation begins at chapter 4 and continues on to the end. Since it commences after the Church period, it is prophetic in nature. Many passages in this division cannot be explained by themselves. As Peter once wrote: "Knowing this first, that no prophecy of scripture is of private interpretation. For no prophecy ever came by the will of man: but men spake from God, being moved by the Holy Spirit" (2 Peter 1.20,21). This simply means no prophecy can be interpreted by its own passage of Scripture. Any attempt to do that is subject to error, for no prophecy is written according to man's will. Had any prophecy been written by the will of man, it would then have been possible for it to be interpreted alone. But this is not the case with prophecies in the Scriptures. Prophecies are given as men are moved by the Holy Spirit. Though the writers are many, the thought is one, because the Holy Spirit is the original author of all these passages on prophecy. Therefore, all prophecies are joined in one. Thus it is essential for anyone wishing to understand prophecy not to interpret it within its own passage of Scripture but to compare it with other biblical passages.

This principle of interpreting Scripture with Scripture is of great importance. The failure of many commentators to accurately handle the word of God can be attributed to the violation of this very principle. "Knowing this first," observed Peter. Any breach of this principle will inevitably cause confusion. How very easy it would be if we could indeed interpret privately. The difficulty created in interpreting Scripture is because correct interpretation always requires that a particular passage agree with the testimony of the whole Bible. Let us consequently study the passages before us by comparing them with other portions of the Scripture so that what we arrive at will not be speculative imaginations but well-founded accurate interpretations.

The Human Image in Daniel

Let us first read Daniel chapter 2. Here we are confronted with a vision or dream of a human image, this particular one of which—in biblical typology—

represents the four Gentile kingdoms. In the King's dream it was subsequently smashed by a stone which became a great mountain that filled the whole earth. This stone is obviously symbolic of the Lord Jesus and His kingdom which will destroy all the kingdoms of the world and replace them on earth. The kingdoms of the earth are not being gradually leavened by the kingdom of God until they finally become God's kingdom. Not at all. These kingdoms will have succeeded one another until they shall suddenly be destroyed by the kingdom of God. The smiting by the stone is of course an event that will occur in the future. We shall shortly come to perceive its relationship with the book of Revelation.

The Beast Images of Daniel

In Daniel chapter 7 it is recorded that the prophet saw another vision which also spoke of the four Gentile kingdoms. The difference between this and what we saw in chapter 2 is that here they are beasts, while there it was a man. The appearing of the kingdom of God was due to the appearing of the Son of man. We are also told even more clearly that the commencement of the kingdom of God is to come after the kingdoms of the earth are at that time destroyed. There will arrive "a little horn" that speaks blasphemously against God and persecutes the elect of God. But his time will only be three years and a half. After that period, the one represented by the little horn shall be destroyed and the Son of man will

come to set up His kingdom. The kingdoms of men
do not coexist with the kingdom of God. Only when
the first are destroyed will the second be set up.

Daniel's Seventy Sevens

Now let us look at Daniel chapter 9. After Daniel
had confessed the sins of his people, God sent Gabriel
to say this to him: "Seventy weeks are decreed upon
thy people and upon thy holy city, to finish transgression, and to make an end of sins, and to make reconciliation for iniquity, and to bring in everlasting
righteousness, and to seal up vision and prophecy,
and to anoint the most holy" (v.24). Since Daniel
prayed to God for His people and His holy city, God
in His answer also mentioned "thy people and thy
holy city." Let us understand that "thy people" points
to the children of Israel, and "thy holy city" refers to
Jerusalem. What God means is this: When the seventy sevens are passed, the transgression of Israel and
the holy city will be finished, their sins will come to
an end, their iniquity will receive reconciliation, and
the everlasting righteousness will be brought to them.
Have all these been fulfilled? No, the children of
Israel continue today to be "Lo-ammi . . . not my
people" (Hosea 1.9). Hence her restoration is yet in
the future. These things still remain unfulfilled
because the prophecy concerning the seventy sevens
has not been fulfilled. But at the second coming of
the Lord Jesus, all the prophecies shall be fulfilled.

"Know therefore and discern," continued Gabriel,
"that from the going forth of the commandment to

restore and to build Jerusalem unto the anointed one, the prince, shall be seven weeks, and threescore and two weeks: it shall be built again, with street and moat, even in troublous times. And after the threescore and two weeks shall the anointed one be cut off, and shall have nothing: and the people of the prince that shall come shall destroy the city and the sanctuary; and the end thereof shall be with a flood, and even unto the end shall be war; desolations are determined" (Dan. 9.25,26). "Troublous times" may also be translated as "brief times." This probably points to the seven sevens, which in terms of time is so much shorter than the sixty-two sevens. The rebuilding of Jerusalem happened within the seven sevens spoken of, which, as calculated by some commentators, come to forty-nine years. Although in the original it merely says "seven"—with no designation of days or years—most commentators believe it refers to the "year" measurement of time, and hence forty-nine years. Sixty-two sevens after the city is rebuilt there shall come the Anointed One.

Here we will not investigate as to when the seventy-sevens actually commenced. One fact is enough for us, however, which is, that we know the Anointed One *did* come after the sixty-nine sevens (seven sevens plus sixty-two sevens). From the time of the decree concerning the rebuilding of Jerusalem to the moment of the coming of the Anointed One, there were to be four hundred eighty-three years. Now that the sixty-nine sevens have already passed and the Anointed One (Christ) has also come, what is left is the last seven. As soon as the last seven is fulfilled the children of Israel will receive the fullness of blessing of Daniel 9.24. However, within the seven years of the death of Christ, was there any day which could have been deemed as a time when transgression was finished for the children of Israel and upon Jerusalem? No, not even a single day. And have there not been over nineteen hundred more years since the time of Christ and still no end of transgression? Hence, it is quite evident that the seventieth seven did not follow immediately after the sixty-nine sevens.

Why is it that this one seven has not been fulfilled and that the children of Israel have not yet received the full blessing? Because "after the threescore and two weeks [the sixty-two sevens mentioned above] shall the anointed one be cut off, and shall have nothing." Christ has died, and consequently the children of Israel did not receive the blessing. It was because they would not receive Him with willing hearts but crucified Him instead, and therefore punishment came upon them. "The people of the prince that shall come shall destroy the city and the sanctuary" (v.26). When the Jews insisted on killing the Lord Jesus, they openly declared: "His blood be on us, and on our children" (Matt. 27.25). Naturally God is treating them according to their own word by temporarily rejecting them and showing grace towards the Gentiles. But after the number of the Gentiles has been fulfilled, He *will* give grace once again to the children of Israel. And at that time, this last seven shall be fulfilled. As soon as the last seven is over, God will deliver the children of Israel according to promise (Dan. 9.24).

"The people of the prince that shall come shall destroy the city and the sanctuary." All students of Revelation know that this refers to the Romans. After the death of Christ the Jews incurred God's severe judgment: the Romans came and destroyed Jerusalem and its temple sanctuary in 70 A.D. Since the term "the people" refers to the Romans, many accordingly think that the term "the prince" obviously points to the Roman prince Titus who led the Romans. But there are many reasons to refute this conclusion. Why is it that the Scripture here does not say the *prince* shall destroy the city but rather says the *people* of the prince? Although the prince must work through his people, it is still unnatural to say the people and not directly say the prince. Since the Holy Spirit mentions both the prince and the people, while nevertheless putting a primary emphasis on the people, can it be that He is implying by this that these people represent the people of that prince who is yet to come? If so, then the prince in question here is not Titus, and the people who attacked Jerusalem in the former day were in spirit and in attitude morally the people of the future prince. This prince whom Daniel prophecies about will be a world renown figure in the future, who is the Antichrist. "The prince that shall come" is therefore the Antichrist.

"The end thereof shall be with a flood, and even unto the end shall be war; desolations are determined" (v.26). "The end" here is not the end of the city nor of the sanctuary. According to correct grammatical construction, "the end thereof" should be connected to the phrase "the prince that shall come."

The fulfillment did not come at the time of Titus but is yet to come in the future. The people of the prince who shall come shall destroy this city and the sanctuary, but "the end thereof" (that is to say, the end of the prince)* shall come as a flood. We know that this superman is soon to come, and the world will have no peace. But thank God, we shall be gone before the Antichrist arrives.

"And he shall confirm a covenant with the many for one week: and in the midst of the week he shall cause the sacrifice and the oblation to cease" (v.27a Darby). The preceding verse tells us of the destructive actions of Antichrist; this next verse continues to speak of his action. The last seven is divided into two halves. At the beginning of the last seven, the Antichrist will confirm a covenant with many. This covenant is not the Old Covenant which God singularly covenanted with His people, for the use of the indefinite article "a" here proves it. The phrase "the many" with the use of the definite article "the" refers to a special group of people—even the Jews. So that this covenant will be a political pact between the Jews and the Antichrist. The duration of the pact is to be seven years, but in the middle of this term of years Antichrist will break it. This is the meaning of the words, "he shall think to change the times and the law," found in chapter 7 and verse 25. Here we may

---

*The Revised Standard Version (1952) recognizes this construction of the verse, as follows: ". . . and the people of the prince who is to come shall destroy the city and the sanctuary. His end shall come with a flood . . ." (9.26 mg.).—*Translator*

see the similarity disclosed between this prince and the little horn mentioned in chapter 7.

In the midst of these seven years in question, Antichrist shall break the covenant, and thus the rest of this period of the seven (that is to say, three years and a half) shall be in his hand. During these three and a half years he shall also wear out the saints (7.25). And during the same three and a half years, this little horn will attempt to change time and season, and cause sacrifice and oblation to cease. At the present moment the Jews have neither sacrifice nor oblation; but in the future these will be restored. We now have seen the beginning of the return of the Jews to Palestine and have also heard of their desire to restore these things. The end is truly near.

Why will the Antichrist cause the sacrifice and the oblation to cease? Because at that time he will speak blasphemously against God (see ch. 7). Since sacrifice and oblation are offered to God, he will naturally forbid them. "And upon the wing of abominations shall come one that maketh desolate; and even unto the full end" (v.27b). "The wing of abominations" speaks of idols. In the temple of God the wings of the cherubim covered the ark. Yet Antichrist shall enter God's temple and proclaim himself God (2 Thess. 2), thus having the wings of abominations. Due to this idolatry, God will permit desolations to extend for three and a half years until the end of the seventy sevens. "And that determined, shall wrath be poured out upon the desolate" (v.27c). The desolate is Jerusalem. As the end of the seventy sevens approaches, the nations shall gather to attack Jerusalem. Then shall the Lord fight for her (Zech. 14.1–6). And so shall the word of Daniel 9.24 be fulfilled.

We may here perceive just how Satan uses man. Antichrist is only a man; but by his obeying Satan he is given devilish power to rule over nations. Though his actual coming is still in the future, nonetheless even in 70 A.D. the Romans had already become Antichrist's people! For they had his spirit. Today we see the many turmoils among the nations. Satan is actually manipulating at the back. He gives power to this person and to that, using many in the political arena as his puppets to disturb the world. The last person he is to use will be the Antichrist. We can even now discern that the spirit of Antichrist is already working everywhere. The most revealing character of the Antichrist is his lawlessness (2 Thess. 2). If we open our eyes to the affairs of this age, we shall know how rampant lawlessness has become. At every level of society there are lawless people. In every profession, the lawless form the majority. It seems as though there is but a thin line between people and the outbreak of lawlessness. Once one yields to lawlessness, that one is forever caught.

For this reason, we who believe in the Lord and are bought with His blood ought at this hour to resist together with one mind Satan and his works both in our spirits as well as in our prayers. Pray that God will enable His Church to know the victory of the cross in order that the saints may have the experience of ascension. The sins of the world need to be judged. The Church of Christ needs to be matured for rapture!

The One Thousand Two Hundred and Sixty Days

Let us examine the last prophecy of Daniel as recorded in chapters 10–12. By carefully examining these chapters we shall see how his last prophecy fits in with his earlier prophecies. I cannot stay to explain it in detail, so let us merely touch upon it briefly.

"And forces shall stand on his part, and they shall profane the *sanctuary*, even the fortress, and shall take away the continual *burnt-offering*, and they shall set up the *abomination that maketh desolate*" (Dan. 11.31). How this coincides indeed with chapter 9. "I heard the man clothed in linen, who was above the waters of the river, when he held up his right hand and his left hand unto heaven, and sware by him that liveth for ever that it shall be for *a time, times, and a half*; and when they have made an end of breaking in pieces the power of the holy people, all these things shall be finished. . . . And from the time that the continual burnt-offering shall be taken away, and the *abomination that maketh desolate* set up, there shall be a thousand two hundred and ninety days. Blessed is he that waiteth, and cometh to the thousand three hundred and five and thirty days. But go thou thy way till the end be; for thou shalt rest, and shall stand in thy lot, at the end of the days" (12.7,11–13). Here we see again the three and a half years' time. One thousand two hundred and ninety days is thirty days more than three and a half years, and a thousand three hundred and thirty-five days is forty-five days more than one thousand two hundred and ninety days. As the three years and a half (1260 days) come to an end, the Lord Jesus will appear on earth. The thirty more days will probably be used to judge the nations (see Matt. 25.31–46), or to cleanse the sanctuary. But after another forty-five days the children of Israel will receive glory.

From the above investigation, we come to know a few things: (1) the time of the Gentiles—that is to say, the time when the Gentiles rule—will come to a sudden end, for One who looks like the Son of man will come with the clouds and set up His kingdom; (2) the last of the Gentile power will be the Roman empire, and its king will speak blasphemously against God and wear out the saints, but he will eventually be judged; (3) the Antichrist will make a covenant with the Jews, and in their unbelief, the latter will restore the sanctuary and its sacrifices; (4) but that after three years and a half, the Antichrist will break the covenant, cause the offering up of sacrifices to cease, and will introduce idolatry; (5) for this reason, desolation will continue to the end of the predetermined period of three and one-half years, and then God will deliver His holy people; and finally (6) the time of the Gentile kingdoms will come to its end with the sudden coming of the Lord from heaven to establish His own kingdom. We have not attempted with any degree of pressure to expound the above Scriptures to suit our own theory, but all we wish to do is to point Scripture to Scripture. We have noticed how the three and a half years of the little horn (ch. 7) fit perfectly with the latter half of the seventieth seven (ch. 9), and also with the three years and a half to be found in chapter 12. And so, the Scriptural prophecies spoken earlier and later agree completely with each other, except that the later prophecy does at times explain the former one or adds to what the former one had not said.

The Prophecy of the Lord Jesus

We have seen how the mind of the Holy Spirit is manifested harmoniously in the Old Testament prophecies. Now let us witness how the prophecies in the New Testament agree with those of the Old, and in addition let us witness how the book of Revelation concurs with all the prophecies of the past. We will look at the Olivet prophecy of our Lord Jesus first; except that for our present purpose we will not delve into all the prophecies given on the Mount of Olives but just those ones which are related to the Jews. We will use Matthew 24 as the basis of our consideration, and use the records in the other Gospels as a further reference. From verse 4 to verse 31 of chapter 24, we read of certain things which pertain to the Jews. We will study this section alongside the prophecies in Daniel in order to obtain a clear understanding.

The disciples asked the Lord Jesus two questions concerning (1) the holy temple and (2) the sign of His coming and of the end of the world (v.3). The question concerning the temple is not relevant to our investigation, and furthermore, it is answered in greater detail in Luke 21. Matthew instead focuses more on the second question. Although with respect to this second question, we find that the disciples mixed up the coming of the Lord with the end of the world, in actuality they are different; nevertheless, we will not deal with the difference since we have limited ourselves to what is relevant to the Jews only.

We should know that the sixty-ninth seven and the seventieth seven are separated by the time of grace. During the last seven the sacrifice and the oblation of the sanctuary will be restored until they are caused to cease by the Antichrist. What our Lord spoke of here refers to that period: "When therefore ye see the abomination of desolation, which was spoken of through Daniel the prophet, standing in the holy place (let him that readeth understand), then let them that are in Judea flee unto the mountains: let him that is on the housetop not go down to take out the things that are in his house: and let him that is in the field not return back to take his cloak" (Matt. 24.15–18).

The latter part of what Jesus said here meant that because the enemy would be in their midst, their flight would therefore be extremely urgent. Since the holy people are the target of the wrath of the Antichrist, and the army of destruction is approaching, it behooves the people to leave everything in order to save their lives. "But woe unto them that are with child and to them that give suck in those days!" (v.19); such is because they are unable to run fast. "And pray ye that your flight be not in the winter, neither on a sabbath" (v.20). This latter statement regarding the sabbath clearly shows its pertinence towards the Jews.

Then the Lord continued by saying, "For then shall be *great tribulation*, such as hath not been from the beginning of the world until now, no, nor ever shall be" (v.21). This word may be linked up with that of Daniel's: "And at that time shall Michael stand up, the great prince who standeth for the children of thy people; and there shall be a time of trouble, such as never was since there was a nation even to that same time: and at that time thy people shall be delivered, every one that shall be found written in the book" (12.1). Those will be days of great tribulation (but they will also be days of the deliverance of God). Consequently, the Lord said: "Except those days had been shortened, no flesh would have been saved: but for the elect's sake those days shall be shortened" (24.22). From the book of Daniel we understand that these days cover three and a half years.

Later on, the Lord spoke of the sign of false christs and false prophets—something which is not found in the Old Testament: "If any man shall say unto you, Lo, here is the Christ, or, Here; believe it not. For there shall arise false Christs, and false prophets, and shall show great signs and wonders; so as to lead astray, if possible, even the elect. Behold, I have told you beforehand. If therefore they shall say to you, Behold, he is in the wilderness; go not forth: Behold, he is in the inner chambers; believe it not. For as the lightning cometh forth from the east, and is seen even unto the west; so shall be the coming of the Son of man. Wheresoever the carcase is, there will the eagles be gathered together" (vv.23–28).

The testimony of Daniel is that as soon as the Anointed One (the Lord Jesus) comes again, all troubles will come to an end. Jesus, as recorded in

Matthew, reports the same thing: "Immediately after the tribulation of those days the sun shall be darkened, and the moon shall not give her light, and the stars shall fall from heaven, and the powers of the heaven shall be shaken: and then shall appear the sign of the Son of man in heaven: and then shall all the tribes of the earth mourn, and they shall see the Son of man coming on the clouds of heaven with power and great glory. And he shall send forth his angels with a great sound of a trumpet, and they shall gather together his elect from the four winds, from one end of heaven to the other" (vv.29–31).

Though briefly discussed, this is enough to show how the prophecies of the New Testament agree with those of the Old.

The Prophecy of Paul (2 Thess. 2.1–11)

Let us inquire into another prophetic passage—this time that of Paul's—and see how it agrees with those prophecies which have just been discussed. "We beseech you, brethren, touching the coming of our Lord Jesus Christ, and our gathering together unto him; to the end that ye be not quickly shaken from your mind, nor yet be troubled, either by spirit, or by word, or by epistle as from us, as that the day of the Lord is just at hand; let no man beguile you in any wise: for it will not be, except the falling away come first, and the man of sin be revealed, the son of perdition, he that opposeth and exalteth himself against all that is called God or that is worshipped; so that he sitteth in the temple of God, setting himself forth as

God" (2 Thess. 2.1–4). What the apostle declares in this prophetic statement is what Daniel meant by "the abomination of desolation" (in the Old Testament, the phrase "the abomination of desolation" means an idol); and we need to recall that the prophecy of the Lord Jesus likewise mentioned this point.

Concerning how the Antichrist of Paul's writing (that is to say, "the man of sin"—"the son of perdition") will exalt himself and resist the Lord, we have already read what Daniel had to say about it. And here is what Paul has to say: "Remember ye not, that, when I was yet with you, I told you these things? And now ye know that which restraineth, to the end that he may be revealed in his own season. For the mystery of lawlessness doth already work: only there is one that restraineth now, until he be taken out of the way. And then shall be revealed the lawless one, whom the Lord Jesus shall slay with the breath of his mouth, and bring to nought by the manifestation of his coming" (vv.5–8). This passage tells the end of the Antichrist. As soon as the Lord Jesus comes again, Antichrist will be judged and destroyed. In his prophecies, Daniel often showed how the Lord will come again to put to nought the powers of the Gentile nations. His narrative of how the little horn is to be destroyed confirms what is said here by Paul in 2 Thessalonians 2.8: the little horn will be destroyed by the appearing of the Lord.

And then the apostle ends his prophecy by saying: "Even he, whose coming is according to the working of Satan with all power and sign and lying wonders, and with all deceit of righteousness for them that perish; because they received not the love of the truth, that they might be saved. And for this cause God sendeth them a working of error, that they should believe a lie: that they all might be judged who believed not the truth, but had pleasure in unrighteousness" (vv.9–12). And what is this lie? John tells us this: "Who is the liar but he that denieth that Jesus is the Christ?" (1 John 2.22)

By means of this brief study we are able to see how the prophecies of the Old Testament and of the New are one and mutually explanatory. Let us therefore take heed of Peter's warning: "No prophecy of scripture is of private interpretation" (2 Peter 1.20). Prophecy must not be interpreted independently within its own narrow passage; it should be proven and confirmed by the entire Bible. Only thus can we arrive at an accurate understanding; otherwise, we shall suffer great loss.

Having seen how the prophecies of both Testaments fit harmoniously together, we can now return more specifically to the book of Revelation and see how it too agrees with all the aforementioned prophecies. In view of Peter's word, we know one thing most assuredly — which is, that the prophecy of the last book of the New Testament must also coincide with these above-mentioned prophecies. We must not take the prophecy given in Revelation out of the context of the entire Bible within which it is a part and attempt to give it a special interpretation. Apart from the first and second divisions of Revelation (ch. 1; and chs. 2 and 3) which relate to the Church, its third division (chs. 4–22) concurs in substance with all the prophecies which we have up to this point examined.

Naturally, being the last book of the Bible, Revelation contains things which are found nowhere else in the preceding books of the Scriptures; nevertheless, in its broad outline, it still cannot be "privately interpreted" but must be proven and confirmed by other Scriptures. According to the key mentioned at the very beginning of our discussion, which key the Holy Spirit has provided us as an aid to interpret its prophecy, we are given to know that all the words in the third division really point to future time and future events. With that as background, then, let us now examine this third division of the book to see how it concurs with the foregoing prophecies.

Third Division of "Revelation" Concurs with the Other Bible Prophecies

We earlier saw that the human image in Daniel's writing symbolizes the time of the Gentile rule. From this image we recognized Babylon, Medo-Persia, Greece, and Rome as signified by the golden head, the silver breasts, the brass belly, and the iron legs. But we know from history that these have all passed away; only the image's ten toes—partly of iron and partly of clay—have yet to be revealed in human history. These ten toes symbolically represent the future confederacy of the *revived* Roman Empire that is to arise. But at the fullness of time, a stone from heaven (which stone, as we saw, points to the Lord Jesus) will break them to pieces and will itself fill the whole earth. Likewise, in Revelation we are told of ten horns (13.1) which stand for ten kings (17.12), representing the last powers of the Gentiles. But "these shall war against the Lamb, and the Lamb shall overcome them, for he is Lord of lords, and King of kings" (17.14). What agreement we find here with Daniel!

In the vision of the beasts in Daniel 7, it is recorded that a little horn came up among the ten horns, and this little horn "shall speak words against the Most High, and shall wear out the saints of the Most High [the Jews]; and he shall think to change the times and the law; and they shall be given into his hand until a time and times and half a time" (v.25). In reading Revelation, we learn of a beast (Daniel's little horn) who is greater than the ten horns (17.12,13) and who speaks blasphemies (13.5) and makes war with the Jews (v.7). He speaks blasphemies against God (v.6) and has authority for forty-two months (v.5). Once again we see the perfect harmony.

Daniel 9 tells us of seventy sevens, of which sixty-nine sevens have already passed but the seventieth seven is yet to come. As the last seven arrives, Antichrist will make a covenant with the children of Israel; but after three and a half years he will break the covenant and set up the idol image which is "the abomination of desolation." The last two chapters of Daniel repeat the mentioning of the setting up of this abomination (11.31 and 12.11). As we have seen, the Lord Jesus himself referred to this matter too, and so did Paul. And when we come to Revelation, we find the same thing: it records how the second beast entices people to make the image of the first beast and to worship it (13.14,15,4,8).

Daniel 9 observes how the Antichrist will break his covenant in the midst of the last seven, which leaves another three years and a half remaining. This coincides with the three and a half years alluded to in Revelation chapter 7 and mentioned directly in Revelation chapter 12, during which time the Antichrist will be in power.

The time of the Antichrist is altogether forty-two months (Rev. 13.5), which is three and a half years' time. During that period the wicked cruelty of the beast and the related idolatry shall be rampant upon the earth. It is then that Jerusalem will be trodden under foot again, that the two men clothed in sackcloth will bear witness, that the persecuted saints will flee to the wilderness to be under the protection of God, and also that the Gentiles shall have dominion on the earth. All these will happen within the three years and a half. Within a very short time afterwards, the Messiah will come to reign.

We have thus seen how the prophecies found in the book of Revelation agree with Daniel's prophecies found in the Old Testament. Now, though, let us learn how they concur with the prophecies of the Lord Jesus.

According to Matthew's record of Jesus' words, the signs of the end are (1) false Christs (24.5; cf. also v.24); (2) wars (vv.6,7); (3) famines (v.7); (4) pestilences (v.7 AV; cf. also Luke 21.11); (5) martyrs (v.9); and (6) signs in the sun, moon and stars (v.29).

By comparing what Matthew's record of Jesus' words says with the six seals spoken of in Revelation, we can readily see the similarities. Even the order of them are the same. Moreover, Jesus in Matthew's account speaks of the "abomination of desolation . . . standing in the holy place" (v.15), but so also does Revelation (13.14,15). In Matthew, our Lord warns the Jews that as soon as they see the idol being set up, they should flee; Revelation too describes how they run (12.6). Matthew records that Jesus says that for the sake of the elect that day will be shortened (24.22); Revelation states: "the devil . . . knowing that he hath but a short time" (12.12). Jesus in Matthew's account states how the false christs and the false prophets shall show great signs and wonders so as to lead astray, if possible, even the elect (24.24); and a similar statement is given in Revelation: "he deceiveth them that dwell on the earth by reason of the signs" (13.14). In Matthew Jesus tells how people will look for an earthly Christ (24.26); Revelation shows how they follow an earthly beast (13.3). Finally, Matthew indicates how the Lord will come from heaven; and Revelation describes how the Lord with His army shall come out of heaven in glory and power (19.11–16).

We should also notice the harmony between Revelation and the Thessalonian prophecy of Paul. Paul mentions the revealing of the man of sin, the son of perdition; Revelation tells of the appearing of the Antichrist (13.1). Paul says the man of sin will oppose the Lord; Revelation records how he blasphemes God (13.6). Paul foretells how that man of sin will exalt himself as God to be worshipped; Revelation describes how he has his image made to receive homage (13.14,15). Paul describes that his coming is according to the working of Satan; Revelation narrates how he receives power from the dragon (that is to say, from Satan) (12.9, 13.4). Paul predicts he will perform signs and lying wonders; Revelation observes that "his death-stroke [will be] healed" (13.3; cf. also v.14). Paul concludes that he will be destroyed by the glory of the coming of the Lord Jesus; Revelation depicts him as being seized at the coming of the Lord and then being "cast alive into the lake of fire that burneth with brimstone" (19.20).

Can we not now see how the prophecies in Revelation correspond so intimately with all the other prophecies in both the Old and New Testaments? How truly one is the word of the Lord! Even as the prophecies quoted above from the New Testament as well as the Old await their fulfillment in the coming days, so also do the corresponding words in Revelation await their future realizations too.

13 | The Other Revelations in the Book of Revelation

We have demonstrated how Revelation supports and reinforces all the other prophecies in the Bible. But Revelation is not limited to merely confirming what was prophesied before, for basically it is not a repeated proclamation of the saying of former prophets. It touches upon many new regions of foretelling which the prophets of old had never known as well as sheds more light on the prophecies of the past. In our study we have discovered how its word concerning the Antichrist coincides perfectly with former prophecies. But now we shall see God's *signs* of judgment in the book of Revelation.

The Bible frequently suggests that signs (not false signs) from *God* are to be the characteristics of the last days: "There shall be great earthquakes, and in diverse places famines and pestilences; and there shall be terrors and great signs from heaven" (Luke 21.11) —"I will show wonders in the heaven above, and signs on the earth beneath; blood, and fire, and vapor of smoke:

the sun shall be turned into darkness, and the moon into blood, before the day of the Lord come, that great and notable day" (Acts 2.19,20).

The book of Revelation tells how God will perform these signs. Once earlier God had made a covenant of marvels with the house of Jacob, and this covenant will be fulfilled during the time of the third division of this book of Revelation: "Behold, I make a covenant: before all thy people I will do marvels, such as have not been wrought in all the earth, nor in any nation [and therefore greater than the signs God had wrought earlier in Egypt]; and all the people among which thou art shall see the work of Jehovah; for it is a terrible thing that I do with thee [for because the Jews are scattered among the nations, these signs will be universal in their manifestation]" (Ex. 34.10). Revelation speaks of how God will use these signs to deliver the Jews.

The sins of the world shall increase by the day until God must *graciously* act. At that moment, the most gracious way of God to deal with the earth's terrible situation is for Him to punish the world: "Wail ye; for the day of Jehovah is at hand; as destruction from the Almighty shall it come. Therefore shall all hands be feeble, and every heart of man shall melt . . . Behold, the day of Jehovah cometh, cruel, with wrath and fierce anger; to make the land a desolation, and to destroy the sinners thereof out of it" (Is. 13.6–9). These signs shall be performed not only to destroy sinners but also to counteract the lying wonders to be done by the Antichrist, thus demonstrating God's own divine character. God is God; Satan is not God. Hence, Revelation records the sores which Satan cannot heal, the earthquakes which Satan cannot stop, the resurrection and rapture which Satan cannot block, and the chains which Satan cannot break. Satan will be no match for God. The signs from heaven shall be more powerful than the wonders from hell. How comforting to know this!

The many signs recorded in Revelation are performed directly by the hand of God. These things are supernatural, and are miracles of God. (Being miracles, they are facts, and therefore have to be accepted literally and not to be spiritualized away.) By comparing Revelation with "the day of Jehovah" or "the day of the Lord" in the Old Testament prophecies, we can discover how harmonious the Bible's last words are with these earlier prophecies.

Obviously, the third division of Revelation touches additionally upon things which will occur after the millennial kingdom, but these are not central to our concerns here and therefore we will not deal with them here.

14 | A Brief Summary Concerning the Things to Come

It might be helpful to conclude with a brief summary of the end-time events. The first thing to come is the rapture of the overcoming believers. All who have the cross wrought deeply in their lives will be raptured. But those who are saved and yet mix with the world and compromise with sins will remain on earth and pass through the Great Tribulation. Only the victorious and watchful saints are ready to be received (the rest of the saved believers will go through the Great Tribulation and be received at the sounding of the seventh trumpet). All this pertains to Christians.

During that time the Roman Empire will be revived, and a very strong person shall be her emperor. He will be given certain powers by Satan in order to perform signs and lying wonders. He will call himself Christ and steal the hearts of many Jews. At that period, the Jews have already returned to their native land, but most of them are unbelievers. They shall rebuild the temple and restore their former worship and sacrifices. Out of fear towards outside powers, they will make a pact with the Antichrist for seven years in order to receive his protection. No doubt, there will still be a remnant who believe in the word of God and oppose the name of the false Messiah.

In the midst of these seven years, there will come forth a sign in heaven, for the red dragon (Satan) will be cast down from heaven to the earth. He will be filled with hatred towards the saints of God—those Jews who bear witness for God. He will stir the heart of the Antichrist—the Roman Emperor—to oppose those Jews.

But just as Satan persecutes those who belong to God, so God will punish those who belong to Satan. The "trumpets" and the "bowls" spoken of in the book of Revelation shall be the manifestations of God's wrath towards the Antichrist and the inhabitants of the earth. In punishing the world, God will still expect them to repent, but the world will persist in evil and will not repent.

Through the power of Satan, the Antichrist will break his covenant, cause all sacrifices and offerings to cease, and will set up the idol image—that wing of abomination—for people to worship. The false prophet will come forth to persuade people to worship the image. As soon as the image is set up, the remnant will immediately flee to the wilderness. Although Satan will use every means to destroy them, God shall take care of them during the three and a half years.

Having no outlet for his wrath, Satan shall turn to persecute those Christian believers who have not previously been raptured. Many will be martyred. But at the sounding of the seventh trumpet, the believers who remain on earth shall also be raptured because they will have learned obedience through sufferings and will have now been perfected.

Then will the Antichrist gather together all nations to come and attack the Jews (the war of Armageddon). The Jews will flee from the city (see Zech. 14). This will happen at the conclusion of the last seven mentioned in Daniel, when the Lord Jesus will come from heaven with His saints and His feet will touch the Mount of Olives. He will save the children of Israel and destroy the nations which war against Him. Then shall commence the millennial kingdom.

Such is a general outline of the book of Revelation. However, those who believe in the Lord and have been *faithful, watching, ready, overcoming,* and *praying* will have already been raptured to heaven before these things shall come upon the world. There will be no need for them to go through the Great Tribulation. Therefore, we need to have the spirit of rapture now. We must have the experience of rapture in spirit before we can find it fulfilled in body. Our spirit should go to heaven first, and then our body will follow suit. May we not be entangled in the things of this world so that we may go when the time comes. The "powers of the age to come" (cf. Heb. 6.5) should be manifested in the lives of the saints today. But, alas, many today seem to fall short.

Lord, will You be gracious? Lead us and keep us that we may seek the truth, that we may have the light of the future to illumine our current course, that we may let the future judgment seat of Christ induce us to judge ourselves at present, and that we may taste the future joy now so as to strengthen our communion with the Spirit of the Lord today. Let us not study this most blessed book as though it were a kind of mental examination, but may the study of it radically change our lives and works. Amen.

15 | A Detailed Outline of "Revelation"

(A) "THE THINGS WHICH THOU SAWEST" (Chapter 1)

(1) Introductory Word	vv.1–3
(2) Greetings and Benediction	vv.4,5
(3) Shout of Joy	vv.5–7
(4) The Testimony of God	v.8
(5) John at Patmos	v.9
(6) The Vision of the Glorious Christ	vv.10–16
(7) The Commission of the Lord	vv.17–20

(B) "THE THINGS WHICH ARE" (Chapters 2,3)

Chapter 2

(1) Ephesus (Post-Apostolic Church)	vv.1–7
(2) Smyrna (Suffering Church)	vv.8–11
(3) Pergamum (Corrupt Church)	vv.12–17
(4) Thyatira (Roman Church)	vv.18–29

Chapter 3

(5) Sardis (Reformed Church)	vv.1–6
(6) Philadelphia (Faithful Little Flock)	vv.7–13
(7) Laodicea (Apostate Church)	vv.14–22

(C) "THE THINGS WHICH SHALL COME TO PASS"
(Chapters 4–22)

1. Vision at the Throne (Chs. 4,5)

Chapter 4
(1) Heaven Opened   v.1
(2) The Throne   vv.2,3
(3) The Twenty-Four Elders   v.4
(4) Conditions around the Throne   vv.5,6
(5) The Four Living Creatures   vv.7,8
(6) Praises   vv.9–11

Chapter 5
(7) "Who Is Worthy to Open the Book?"   vv.1–4
(8) The Lion—the Lamb   vv.5–7
(9) The Praise of the Living Creatures and
       the Twenty-Four Elders   vv.8–10
(10) The Praise of the Angels and the Creation   vv.11–14

2. Opening of Seven Seals (Chs. 6–8.5)

Chapter 6
(1) The First Seal—White Horse   vv.1,2
(2) The Second Seal—Red Horse   vv.3,4
(3) The Third Seal—Black Horse   vv.5,6
(4) The Fourth Seal—Pale Horse   vv.7,8
(5) The Fifth Seal—The Cry under the Altar   vv.9–11
(6) The Sixth Seal—The Shaking of Heaven
       and Earth   vv.12–1

The Vision That Is Inserted between the Sixth
    and Seventh Seals (Chapter 7)

Chapter 7
(1) The Israeli Remnant   vv.1–8
(2) The Saved among the Gentiles   vv.9–17

End of the Inserted Vision

Chapter 8
(7) The Seventh Seal   vv.1,2
(8) Condition in Heaven after the Seventh Seal   vv.3–5

3. Blowing of the Seven Trumpets (Chs. 8.6–11.19)

(1) The First Trumpet   vv.6,7
(2) The Second Trumpet   vv.8,9
(3) The Third Trumpet   vv.10,11
(4) The Fourth Trumpet   vv.12,13

Chapter 9
(5) The Fifth Trumpet—The First Woe   vv.1–12
(6) The Sixth Trumpet—The Second Woe   vv.13–21

The Vision Inserted between the Sixth and
    Seventh Trumpets (Chs. 10–11.14)

Chapter 10
(1) The Strong Angel   vv.1–7
(2) The Little Book   vv.8–11

Chapter 11
(3) The Temple and the Altar   vv.1,2
(4) The Two Witnesses   vv.3–12
(5) A Great Earthquake   vv.13,14

End of the Inserted Vision

(7) The Seventh Trumpet   vv.15–18
(8) Condition in Heaven after the Seventh
       Trumpet   v.19

4. The Triune Satan (Chs. 12,13)

Chapter 12
(1) The Great Sign   vv.1–5
(2) The Fleeing of the Woman   v.6
(3) The War in Heaven   vv.7–9
(4) A Great Voice   vv.10–12
(5) The Dragon Persecuting the Woman   vv.13–17

122 *Aids to Revelation*

10. The Last Warning (Ch. 22.6–end)

(1) The Message of the Angel	vv.6–11
(2) The Message of the Lord	vv.12,13
(3) Two Kinds of People	vv.14,15
(4) Christ's Own Testimony	v.16
(5) The Response of the Holy Spirit and the Bride	v.17
(6) The Last Warning	vv.18,19
(7) The Last Message, Prayer and Blessing	vv.20,21